THE SHOOTING SCRIPT

BLACK HAWK DOWN

SCREENPLAY AND INTRODUCTION BY
KEN NOLAN

FOREWORD BY
MARK BOWDEN

A Newmarket Shooting Script® Series Book

NEWMARKET PRESS • NEW YORK

FIRST EDITION

02   03   04   10   9   8   7   6   5   4   3   2   1

ISBN: 1-55704-530-5 (paperback)

Library of Congress Catalog-in-Publication Data is available upon request.

QUANTITY PURCHASES
Companies, professional groups, clubs, and other organizations may qualify for special terms when ordering quantities of this title. For information, write to Special Sales, Newmarket Press, 18 East 48th Street, New York, NY 10017; call (212) 832-3575 or 1-800-669-3903; FAX (212) 832-3629; or e-mail mailbox@newmarketpress.com.

Website: www.newmarketpress.com

Manufactured in the United States of America.

★*Includes Screenplay*

CONTENTS

FOREWORD

BY MARK BOWDEN

I first met Jerry Bruckheimer in his Santa Monica office in January 1998. There was lots of exposed brick. He sat behind a polished wooden desk long enough to make a good start on a bowling lane. A huge German Shepherd prowled the office, and before me on his desk was a collection of colorful, expensive fountain pens.

Jerry is a small, slender, precise man who usually dresses in dark colors. His office was intimidating, but he wasn't.

I knew of him, of course. He was the impresario of loud, upbeat, visually spectacular, buffo box office films like *Top Gun* and *The Rock*, movies that were like super comic books, and since I'd loved comic books from an early age, I'd always enjoyed them. Jerry had just purchased the rights to my book *Black Hawk Down*, which was in all but superficial ways the opposite of a Bruckheimer film. It was about a battle, so it had a lot of noise, violence, and confusion, but the book was also serious, dark, and disturbing.

Jerry acknowledged this. He admitted that the project was something of a departure for him, but said that it built on his strengths and experience. He knew how to make action movies work, and he had worked successfully with the Pentagon in past projects—given the modern weaponry involved, particularly the Black Hawk helicopters, military cooperation would be essential to making the film authentic. He told me he really wanted to make the movie, and wanted me to stay involved from beginning to end.

"Have you ever written a screenplay before?" he asked.

When I heard the word, "No," come out of my mouth, I expected a look of surprise or alarm.

Instead, Jerry offered me some broad advice—"Every scene should advance the story, and should end in a way that propels you into the next scene," and "You can lose an audience very quickly if you confuse them or bore them, and once that happens, you can't get them back." He gave me books about screenplay writing and various drafts of scripts that showed how they had progressed through development.

"Whatever happens as we go forward with this, I want to keep you involved through the whole process," he said. "On a movie of this scope, I guarantee you we will bring in five or six screenwriters before we're finished. I would like to see this movie made, so don't get frustrated or impatient about the process. In my experience, movies don't get made because I give up on them, it's because the writers give up."

I had no intention of giving up, nor was I completely naïve about my role in the process. In large part, I was being given the opportunity to participate because *Black Hawk Down* is a true story, one that few people outside secret military units knew as much about as I did. The subject matter was sensitive. The book (and now film) tells the story of a terrifying, pitched 15-hour-long battle fought by elite American soldiers in Mogadishu, Somalia. Eighteen young Americans were killed in that fight, along with an estimated 500 to 1,000 Somalis. At that point, the battle was only five years old. For those who had lost sons, husbands, brothers, and fathers, wounds had not completely healed. And the battle had been a pivotally important episode in modern American history—hardly the stuff of even stylish, light-hearted Hollywood treatment. Images of dead American soldiers being dragged through the streets of that African city by enraged mobs were some of the most disturbing in our nation's history. The material needed to be treated with respect. Jerry wanted me involved, I knew, because, as the book's author, I could help bridge the gap between big-budget entertainment and history.

Frankly, I discounted much of what he told me. They needed me, I figured, so they were going to humor me. They were going to let me attempt the script, pay me well, and then get down to serious work.

But the deal suited me perfectly. *Black Hawk Down* was the third story I had sold to Hollywood. The first was an article I wrote for *Rolling Stone* magazine that had never made it out of development. The second, a magazine series I wrote for *The Philadelphia Inquirer*, had been made into the film *Money for Nothing*, starring John Cusack. I was not given a chance to work on the scripts for either movie, and the one that got made had departed from the original story in ways that I hadn't particularly liked. In both projects, I noticed that screenwriters had been paid extremely well to prepare scripts—most of which had been discarded. I figured if somebody was going to get paid well to adapt one of my stories into a screenplay that would just wind up in the trashcan, it might as well be me. I had nothing to lose and everything to gain. If I wrote a terrible script, I would get paid handsomely, and they would hire a real screenwriter for the job. But if I wrote a passable script, I not only might affect how the movie got made, I might open the door to more work on films.

I spent much of the summer of 1998 drafting my first screenplay, figuring out how to collapse the chaotic events of that battle, and the actions of more than 60 or more characters, into a tightly-structured, two-hour drama centering on a handful of main characters. I knew that authors were often too protective of their books, and tended to produce overly literal adaptations that were too ponderous and wordy for the screen, so I liberally departed from mine, inventing scenes and dialogue that fleshed out composite characters, trying more to capture the book's spirit than adhere faithfully to the real events. By the end of the summer I had played the drama through in my head from beginning to end seamlessly. It portrayed most of the major events of the battle, and captured the personalities, jargon, courage, and style of the small corps of Rangers and Delta Force operators whom I had come to know and like so much while researching the book.

I will never forget the first response I received from Chad Oman, one of the film's executive producers, after turning the script in.

"Well, Mark," he said on the telephone from Los Angeles. "To tell you the truth, we weren't expecting too much from this first draft, and we're pleasantly surprised. *We might even be able to use some of this.*"

Proud moments, I suppose, come in different shapes and sizes. If I sent a manuscript to my editor in New York, and he had called to tell me "We might even be able to use some of this," it would be a devastating blow. Chad's reaction meant that I had not completely wasted my time.

The real task of writing the movie *Black Hawk Down* was then turned over to Ken Nolan.

I found him to be a young man with boundless energy and obsessive work habits. I prefer to write on a regular schedule, usually before the keyboard for several hours each morning. Ken is a procrastinator. He will agonize over a project for weeks without writing a word, then lock himself in his office, put on movie soundtracks to set the mood, and write in a marathon push, often through several nights and days. Ken was one of those Hollywood stealth successes, writers who make a good living but whose scripts never seem to actually become films.

I met him for the first time on a trip to Hollywood in the summer of 1999, after *Black Hawk Down* had been published and had become a bestseller. Ken showed up at my hotel with a copy of my book that he had turned black with fingerprints, underlinings, and notations. He had a million questions and took extensive notes of all my answers. It was deeply flattering. I had grown used to meeting fans of the book, even some who knew it quite well, but I had never met anyone like Ken. The man had *inhaled* my book. As we talked, it was clear to me that he had working knowledge of it that in some ways challenged my own. He is also a man of large enthusiasm.

"Mark, this one is going to actually get *made*," he said. "I'm so excited—honest to God—if they want me to write flying monkeys into it I'll do it."

He was kidding. In the years since, true to Bruckheimer's word, the script went through many drafts. It was reworked by Oscar®-winning screenwriters Steve Zaillian (*Schindler's List*) and Eric Roth (*Forrest Gump*). The prize-winning playwright/actor Sam Shepard, who in the film plays the American commander, Major Gen. William F. Garrison, reworked some of the scenes, and director Ridley Scott even resurrected some of the scenes and dialogue from my original, but the script has remained primarily Ken's. We talked often by phone. We teased each other about what might happen if we actually reached for one of the fancy fountain pens in Bruckheimer's office—"I think that's why he keeps the dog," said Ken.

It was from Ken that I first learned Ridley Scott was considering directing the film. The screenwriter lives in a house directly behind the acclaimed director, so on the day his script was delivered, Ken could actually watch as the messenger knocked on Scott's door and the director accepted the package.

"Ridley Scott was in the doorway holding my script in *his hands*," Ken told me on the phone that night. That the director of *Blade Runner, Alien, Thelma and Louise,* and *Gladiator* might make our film seemed too good to be true. I own only about 30 films on DVD, and the four listed above are among them.

Ridley's interest in the project was, simply, the best thing that could have happened. His previous film, *Gladiator*, had won an Oscar for Best Picture, among others, and had been a huge box office success. He was not just a director known for making beautiful, serious, even great films, but one of the most commercially successful in the world. If he wanted to make the movie, it meant the movie would not only get made, but that no expense would be spared.

"*This*," said Chad Oman, as we filed out of our first extended meeting with Ridley, "is as cool as it gets. Even here!"

That meeting was in Bruckheimer's office in September 2000. Ridley was a fit man with a pink complexion, a short-cropped gray beard, and an ever-present massive Cuban cigar. Gruff, blunt, unassuming, profane, and a delightful raconteur, he entertained us with stories of his travels and moviemaking, and peppered me with questions about the battle itself. Why were U.S. soldiers in Somalia? What was Aidid like? Garrison? How badly destroyed was Somalia? How did the mission get so bollixed up? He spent the better part of a weekend chewing me like the end of one of his cigars.

Ridley had read my screenplay for the film, and wanted to resurrect some of the scenes I had written with Somali characters. We all agreed that the movie, like the book, was primarily a story about American soldiers told through their eyes, but Ridley was determined to convey that the enemy they faced that day was sophisticated and smart, and had legitimate motivations of its own.

On my next trip to L.A., just two months later, Ridley had already picked a neighborhood in Rabat, Morocco, to shoot the film, and his art director, Arthur Max, was already constructing models of the sets. This was going to be Ridley's third major film in less than three years—he had just finished work on *Hannibal*. From the day Ridley signed on, discussion of the project shifted from the abstract to the real.

"The biggest part of directing is being able to make decisions," Ridley says.

They were ready to shoot the film just four months later. I visited the set in April, when the Defense Department delivered on its promise to deploy real army Rangers and pilots from the 160th Special Operations Aviation Regiment to assist with stunts. I had spent years working to re-create in words the raid these units had made on the target house in Mogadishu in 1993, and I had a vivid picture of it in my mind. In Morocco I was able for the first time to actually witness it—the AH-6 Little Birds sweeping suddenly over a crowded street, a warning rattle of machine guns and the crowds fleeing in panic, the choppers dropping right down to the street, kicking up great storms of dust, and the Delta operators leaping off benches into action. Then the bigger, more powerful Black Hawks moving in behind them, ropes dropping from the sides through the cyclone of dust, and Rangers roping suddenly to the street. It was just as I had imagined it, only much more sudden, violent, and loud.

What viewers see in the film is without question the most authentic depiction of modern soldiering ever filmed. Ken's script adheres closely to the actual events of October 3, 1993. It shows how the force was slowed when a young Ranger missed the rope and plunged 70 feet to the dirt street, landing with severe injuries, and how the delay gave a rallying Somali militia the time to amass in sufficient force to pin down the assaulters and shoot down two of its helicopters. Some journalists and critics have labored mightily to find the political message of the film, but there isn't one. At heart, it is the story of a group of young soldiers who desperately want to experience battle and who get their wish. The best stories are not those that lecture us about politics or history, but which connect with us on a visceral level. They connect us with human experience that we otherwise would never know or understand. That was my goal when I wrote the book, and it became Jerry's, Ken's, and Ridley's goal as well. *Black Hawk Down* puts you alongside soldiers in the midst of a horrific battle. No one who reads it or sees it will ever think of combat or of soldiers again in the same way.

On the set in Morocco, in addition to an official Defense Department liaison officer, Bruckheimer hired two former army officers who had served as commanders during the battle itself, Air Commander Lt. Col. Tom Matthews and Delta Force Lt. Col. Lee Van Arsdale. Most of the military stunts performed in the film, from flying choppers to roping Rangers, were performed by actual members of those army units—in some instances, soldiers who had fought in the battle themselves.

"People will see this and say, 'Wow, what amazing CGI [computer-generated imagery],'" said Ridley. "But, as you see, this is all the real thing."

By the end, my own role in the project was reduced to that of gaping with wonder. As I drove to the set each day, I passed thousands of Somali extras lining up for their daily breakfast and pay. A huge swath of Rabat was cordoned off as if under military assault. On the set, hundreds of crew members raced around intently, moving people into position, getting lights, cameras, microphones, smoke-machines, wind-machines, and other tools of their trade in place, while actors like Tom Sizemore, Josh Hartnett, Eric Bana, Jason Isaacs, Ewan McGregor, and others lounged in the shadows, awaiting their few moments on camera that day. Executive producer Mike Stenson, who lived on the set during all the filming, orchestrated this mammoth undertaking every day: coping with complaints from the Moroccan government and police; helping with the creative and personal issues of actors, crew members, their agents, and families; negotiating compromises between the military advisors, Ken, Ridley, and Jerry; and dealing with the million petty problems that arise daily whenever nearly 600 Americans decamp in a foreign land for four solid months.

For me, it was all a little hard to believe. I wandered from set to set, sometimes with Jerry, who was busy shooting still photos of the various remarkable scenes. Ridley was the field general, calmly supervising the final product from a moving headquarters—sometimes inside a tent, sometimes in a garage off the main streets, sitting before an array of a dozen monitors, puffing his cigar, and orchestrating the camera placement and composition on every camera for every shot. His legs are too short to reach the ground from his perch on his director's chair, so he would slide the water cooler over to prop up his boots, patiently lifting them every time someone walked in from the dusty streets looking for a drink. He remained as calm and self-assured as a factory foreman supervising a daily run of widgets. In-between scenes, he spent a lot of time talking to me about our shared passion for tennis.

To me, the pleasure and excitement of the whole experience was crystallized in a moment. On the first day I visited the set, I was given the ride of my life.

"Do you want to ride back on a chopper?" one of the 160th pilots asked.

I assumed he meant riding back from the remote set in the back of a Black Hawk, and I quickly agreed. Two crew chiefs then outfitted Ken and I in harnesses, which surprised me. Black Hawks are big helicopters, with lots of room in the back, and plenty of things to hang onto. Word spread that the writers were going to be given rides, so the actors began clamoring to be included. Ken and I stood looking foolish in our harnesses as the chopper crews began herding them into Black Hawks. I noticed than none of the actors had been similarly fitted.

"Why do we have harnesses on, and they don't?" I asked.

"Oh, you guys aren't going on a Black Hawk," the pilot said. "You guys get to ride back on the pods."

The pods turned out to be the benches on the outside of the MH-6 Little Birds helicopters, the small attack aircraft flown by the 160th Special Operations Aviation Regiment. There is room inside the small chopper for only a pilot and copilot, so the Delta Force operators sit on the pods, flat benches on the *outside* of the airframe. I don't know what Ken was thinking when he heard this, but I experienced panic. All my life I have been panicked by heights. I have a hard time climbing a ladder to do home repairs. The idea of taking a flight on a flat bench on the outside of a moving helicopters terrified me, but given the circumstances, in front of everyone, I was not going to back down.

The harness proved to be a small comfort. It was attached to the outside of the Little Bird by a single strap that had about three feet of play in it. The bench itself had a single, thin plastic strap across it tightly. I worked my fingers under the strap, which was the only handhold. If I were to slip off the bench, which seemed almost likely to me, I would be dangling underneath the chopper high above the ground.

"How long are we going to be up?" I asked the chopper crewman who took a seat on the bench alongside me.

"We should get a good ride tonight; we'll be up about 20 minutes," he said.

We lifted off in formation, with Ken on the bench on the chopper before mine. He was holding a video camera and waving happily. I was doing deep breathing exercises.

We flew toward the sunset, a glowing orange dome that melted to a line of gold at the edge of a sapphire sea, the choppers moving in silhouette before and behind me. The pressure of the air sweeping along the sides of the Little Bird gently pinned me against the side. Once I realized that I would have to actually work to slide off the bench, I began to relax and enjoy. We banked gently left, and flew along the sand cliffs of the coastline of Rabat, and turned back in over the city, where the sky inland turned from deep purple to black. The lights of the city flickered beneath my feet as the formation made a slow swing around the steeple of a mosque. It was magnificent. I felt like a character in *The Arabian Nights*, aloft on a flying carpet.

I left the set well before shooting was finished. Once or twice over the summer, Ridley's office called to ask me to add a few lines of dialogue to key scenes, usually those dealing with the Somali characters or those where General Garrison provides an occasional overview of the chaotic proceedings. Ken was rewriting the same scenes. Ridley would then mix and match from the various drafts, looking for just the right lines to flesh out the action.

Ridley continued to tinker with the film up until the day it premiered. In late September, he asked me to fly out to Hollywood, primarily to help write the text crawls that open and end the film. I worked at the studio for about two weeks. For such an accomplished, established director, Ridley is almost alarmingly open to reactions and suggestions. One day he showed me a sequence of scenes, and, chatting with him about them afterwards, I said I thought it might be interesting to reverse the order—it might have more impact. Ridley promptly asked his film editor, Pietro Scalia, to try it. We watched again, and Ridley announced that he liked the reversed scenes better. I was alarmed. *My god*, I thought, *don't listen to me—you're Ridley Scott!*

The film was all but finished by September 11, when the terrorist attacks on New York and Washington so dramatically altered the political context for stories about the U.S. military. I saw the whole film for the first time on October 3, coincidentally on the eighth anniversary of the battle. Ridley, Jerry, Chad, Mike, and I sat with Joe Roth and other top Revolution Studios executives in their screening room. At the end, Roth stood up and said, in so many words, "It's an amazing movie. I think we ought to bring this out sooner rather than later."

In the final weeks before the film's release, Ridley and Jerry wrestled with the text crawl at the end of the film. At their request, I had written several lines tying the events of October 1993 with was happening in the winter of 2001—the same units involved in the battle of Mogadishu were then fighting in Afghanistan. We all felt—I had written about this in the epilogue to the book—that the Mogadishu battle had prompted not just a sudden end to the mission in Somalia, but a withdrawal of American military force from the world. The world had paid a terrible price for that—in Rwanda, Bosnia, and Kosovo. Even the attacks in New York and Washington were connected, in that the Clinton administration had not forcefully gone after Osama bin Laden and al Qaeda after the 1999 bombings of U.S. embassies in Kenya and Tanzania.

For some of the early screenings, the end crawl drew the connection quite literally. We all decided, finally, to delete the lines. It was better to leave such connections to the viewers' imagination. Ultimately, *Black Hawk Down* is a story about combat. It is about soldiers at war, any war, anywhere, any time. Ending the film with such a stark political message was out of synch with the spirit of the project—both book and film.

For me, the experience of the film has been nothing short of astonishing, exactly the opposite of what authors expect. Few things in my life have been as satisfying as watching so many talented people, so much intelligence and energy, invested in a project that, for me, began with an idea in my kitchen in rural Pennsylvania six years ago. The experience was been lucrative, creatively rewarding, and it gave me more opportunities to work in Hollywood. To some extent it has demystified the process of filmmaking, but I still haven't completely shaken the voice inside my head that reminds me from time to time, with the wide-eyed enthusiasm of the true fan: *You're sitting here working on scenes with Jerry Bruckheimer and Ridley Scott!*

I try not to let it show too much, but I hope I never lose it.

INTRODUCTION

BY KEN NOLAN

I used to run the 3,000-meter race on the high school track team—basically, a two-mile sprint. I was not very good at it. During the middle of every race, I would inevitably begin to fantasize about "having an accident," so I wouldn't have to finish the hellish experience. I needed something that looked plausible to the audience in the stands: tumbling into another racer and landing in a tangled heap of limbs; tripping over my own feet and crashing painfully to the track—letting out an anguished cry of "frustration" as I went down; careening into the bleachers like an out of control Indy 500 car, arms pinwheeling for balance as my head smacked into the grandstand, to the horror of friends and relatives. Of course, I never did any of these things. I endured the burning pain in my lungs and legs, and finished the race.

During the two and a half years of adapting Mark Bowden's book, writing 24 drafts, I often fantasized about having "accidents" so I wouldn't have to go on. Not that I didn't love the story—I read Mark's book five times—it's just that I was really worn out by the, oh, twelfth draft, say, and I fantasized about smashing my car into a telephone pole, contracting Lyme disease from a hike in the San Gabriel Mountains, or drowning in a tragic canoeing accident—anything to keep from doing yet another draft of the script. "Did you hear?" "Hear what?" "Nolan's doctor called this morning. The kid has some kind of rare finger-eating hantavirus." "No!" "Yep. Can't write. Hell, he can't *type*. Got no fingers. We gotta get someone else to do the next draft."

Instead, I stayed on the project (in fact, was lucky to be working on it), taking extensive development notes from Ridley Scott, Jerry Bruckheimer, and Exec Producers Mike Stenson and Chad Oman. Every draft we worked on, we learned something new. Some drafts got much better, and some we made worse. We'd have meetings and say, "Well, *that* didn't work...let's go back to what we had before...but this time let's try *this*..." It was a process of trial and error.

I came to realize that a script is never finished. It will never be perfect. The only reason it will be "done" is because there's nothing left to work on. Once, when we were having one of our umpteenth meetings on the tenth draft, I muttered something like: "Is this ever going to end?" Chad Oman looked at me and said, "It'll end the day we stop filming." I shrunk in my seat and muttered, "Oh."

I didn't know any better. Until that time, I had never written a produced script. I had never even been to a real film set. And yet, for four years I had been paid as a professional screenwriter. I had sold three scripts to studios, adapted a nonfiction book, and worked on various assignments. My friends and family considered me a "successful" screenwriter. I knew better. None of my scripts had been made into movies. I was starting to worry. I knew I needed to get a movie made. But I didn't want to write just anything. I took meeting after meeting, where I was offered the material that had somehow trickled down from the A-list screenwriters. Most of it was not good. In fact, 98 percent of it stunk.

Then, in the summer of 1998, at one of these meetings that usually amount to nothing, producer Todd Garner gave me the galleys of a new book called *Black Hawk Down*. I had no idea what the title meant. What was a "Black Hawk" anyway? Todd said, "Remember that time a few years back on CNN when the dead American soldier was being dragged through the streets of that African city with a rope tied around his legs?" I said, "Oh, yeah. I do remember that. Where was that?" Todd smiled, "Read this. That's what the book is about."

I took the book home, got into bed that night, and started reading. By page 10 I knew I was reading something incredible. Something powerful, unexpected, and gut-wrenching. I *had* to write the script. I met with Jerry Bruckheimer's executives a week later and somehow weaseled my way into the job.

Cut to: a year-and-a-half later, when we were developing draft number 12, and I was fantasizing about industrial accidents—getting my typing fingers caught in an out-of-control Slurpee machine, getting swept into a roaring and vengeful dry cleaning press, or being inflated to grotesque proportions by an automatic balloon pump. I knew one writer who got out of an assignment when his house burned down. Could I burn mine down? How much time would that really buy me?...

Why did it take so long to develop the script? Mark Bowden's incredibly detailed book had over 60 real-life characters to chose from. Each soldier who fought on October 3, 1993, had a story to tell. An amazing story. Each one. We had to pick which stories to use, and which characters' points of view to show the movie from.

Hydra-like questions arose every time we changed something in the script. A dozen problems would crop up each time we altered a storyline. Domino-effect problems plagued us draft after draft. How much time should we spend on the Lost Convoy story? How often should we cut back to General Garrison in the Joint Operations Center? How much time do we spend in the first act getting to know the guys? What does Sergeant Eversmann learn during his trial by fire? How do we retain the ensemble nature of the story without distancing the audience with a cold retelling of history, without characters to empathize with and get to know? How much politics do we put in the film without boring the audience?

During our marathon development meetings there was an unspoken gargoyle looming over all of us in the room. We knew that this was an important story. None of us wanted to disrespect the memories of the brave soldiers who fought and died on the streets of Mogadishu. None of us wanted to make a mediocre film that would somehow trivialize what the soldiers did. But we also knew that we were, in the end, making a *movie*. Some things simply had to be changed or they wouldn't make sense to the viewer. Some characters had to do things that other real-life characters did. Some storylines had to be truncated, others expanded, and some slightly fictionalized.

After working for so long on the project, Mark's story became "my" story, too. I developed an emotional attachment to the script. I knew every character, every storyline inside and out. And I worried about what the families of the soldiers would think when they saw the film. I knew it would be a painful experience for them, especially if their son, husband or brother was killed on October 3, 1993. This weighed heavily on my mind. I imagined these families psyching themselves up to see the film, or avoiding it altogether. I knew—I think we all knew—we had a big responsibility.

Every time I sat down to write, I reminded myself that I wanted to make the story as realistic as possible, but also deliver a piece of entertainment that would grip readers by the throat for two and a half hours and not let them go. This was a very difficult balance to find.

Underneath all this was my main concern—moving the story along at a breakneck pace. I do not believe a script is merely a "blueprint" to a film. The script is its own entity, separate from the final motion picture. When you read a good script, you don't realize you're turning the page to see what happens next. When you read a bad script, turning a page is like trying to pull a manhole cover up with your fingertips. I wanted every draft of the script to read the way Mark's book did for me the first time I read *Black Hawk Down*—an incredibly visceral story that kept me turning the pages and wondering what would happen next. I wanted my script to be as remembered as the film would be. I knew this was a silly idea—after all, how many people actually *read* scripts? But I held onto the belief that the script is not just a blueprint. I still believe that.

The script was not a blueprint, and I was not an architect. That was not my job. My job wasn't "screen-architect," it was "screen*writer*." My job was to thrust the reader onto the streets of Mogadishu, and keep him or her there. My job was to make the reader care about the characters, and to keep turning the pages. With each draft, the script should have been an amazing reading experience.

I hope we accomplished that. You read the screenplay and decide for yourself.

BLACK HAWK DOWN

Screenplay
by
Ken Nolan

Based on the Book
by
Mark Bowden

FADE IN:

SUPER: BASED ON AN ACTUAL EVENT

SUPER: ALL OUR IGNORANCE BRINGS US NEARER TO DEATH. T.S. ELLIOT

EXT. DESERT - DAY

A Somalian man hunches over a body wrapped in a sheet and covers the dead man's face.

SUPER: SOMALIA 1992

The images of a lonely truck driving through ravaged countryside, bodies everywhere.

SUPER: YEARS OF WARFARE AMONG RIVAL CLANS CAUSES FAMINE ON A BIBLICAL SCALE.

We now see that the truck is from the Red Cross as it moves through the ruins of a bombed and burned village. Past bodies -- some dead, some alive. No sound but the wind. Nothing else moves across scorched earth.

SUPER: 300,000 CIVILIANS DIE OF STARVATION.

SUPER: MOHAMED FARRAH AIDID, THE MOST POWERFUL OF THE WARLORDS, RULES THE CAPITAL MOGADISHU.

A body wrapped in a sheet is carried away.

SUPER: HE SEIZES INTERNATIONAL FOOD SHIPMENTS AT THE PORTS. HUNGER IS HIS WEAPON.

SUPER: THE WORLD RESPONDS. BEHIND A FORCE OF 20,000 U.S. MARINES, FOOD IS DELIVERED AND ORDER IS RESTORED.

A U.N. Peacekeeper helps a wearied man drink.

SUPER: APRIL 1993

SUPER: AIDID WAITS UNTIL THE MARINES WITHDRAW, AND THEN DECLARES WAR ON THE U.N. PEACEKEEPERS.

The Peacekeeper walks past the bodies of dead children.

SUPER: IN JUNE, AIDID'S MILITIA AMBUSH AND SLAUGHTER 24 PAKISTANI SOLDIERS, AND BEGIN TARGETING AMERICAN PERSONNEL.

Lifeless refugees are drawn to the aid station.

SUPER: IN LATE AUGUST, A COMPANY OF AMERICA'S ELITE

(CONTINUED)

CONTINUED:

        SOLDIERS, DELTA FORCE AND ARMY RANGERS, ARE SENT TO
        MOGADISHU TO REMOVE AIDID AND RESTORE ORDER.

Looking out at the smoldering, wind-whipped village from
inside a bomb-ravaged house.

TITLE: BLACK HAWK DOWN

EXT. HIGH ABOVE MOGADISHU - DAY

The first rays of sunshine hit us -- and a BLACK HAWK
HELICOPTER thunders over the arid Somali landscape.

SUPER: SATURDAY - OCTOBER 2, 1993

INT. BLACK HAWK HELICOPTER - SAME

A handsome Ranger, SERGEANT MATT EVERSMANN, surveys the
village below.

EXT. HIGH ABOVE MOGADISHU - SAME

A make-shift camp surrounding a bombed-out building on a
hilltop bustles with energy.

SUPER: RED CROSS FOOD DISTRIBUTION CENTER

EXT. MOGADISHU STREETS - CONT.

Several "Technicals", old Toyota trucks with heavy machine
gun bolted in back, ROAR through the village.

Starving residents swarm a five-ton Red Cross transport truck
loaded with food as the Black Hawk floats slowly past.

The scene turns chaotic: villagers shake the truck; Somali
soldiers beat them back with sticks; ten-pound sacks of wheat
spill onto the ground; hordes of stick-thin villagers
struggle to grab the sacks.

A Somali GUNMAN OPENS FIRE on the mob. Blood splatters as a
few get hit. Screams. Panic. People scatter.

INT. DURANT'S SUPER SIX FOUR BLACK HAWK - SAME

MATT EVERSMANN jolts from the sight of the bloodbath. Whips
inside to the other RANGERS in the Black Hawk's belly.

                EVERSMANN
        Oh shit, did you see that?
           (into headset)
        Chief, we got unarmed civilians getting
        shot down here at nine o'clock!

CONTINUED:

Durant surveys the scene below, then calmly speaks into his
headset.

                    DURANT
          I got it Matt, I don't think we can touch
          this.

Heavily armed Militiamen train weapons on the populace. One
shouts into a megaphone:

                    MILITIA MAN
               (in Somali, subtitled)
          This food is the property of Mohammed
          Farrah Aidid! Go back to your homes!

Durant's Black Hawk circles the village.

                    DURANT
          Command, Super Six Four we got militia
          shooting unarmed civilians down at the
          food distribution center. Request
          permission to engage.

                    MATTHEWS (V.O.)
          Super Six Four, are you taking fire,
          over?

Somali Militia men flee into the crowd as Delta sniper SGT.
DAN BUSCH trains his AR-15 rifle on the gunmen below.

                    DURANT
          Negative, Command.

                    MATTHEWS (V.O.)
          U.N.'s jurisdiction, Six Four. We can't
          intervene. Return to base. Over.

                    DURANT
               (frustrated)
          Roger. Six Four returning.

Durant continues the chopper away from the village.

ON EVERSMANN - staring down at the carnage-strewn streets
below. He can't believe it.

BELOW - The militia man aims his megaphone at the Black Hawk
as though he's firing a gun at it.

EXT. HIGH OVER NORTH MOGADISHU - DAY

SUPER: NORTH MOGADISHU

BAKARA MARKET

AIDID CONTROLLED TERRITORY

EXT. MOGADISHU MARKET - DAY

The market bustles with activity. Militia men stroll the
streets, automatic rifles strapped across their backs.

HOOT slinks through the crowd, following a Somali DRIVER.

INT. MOGADISHU MARKET - CONTINUOUS

OSMAN ATTO, a wealthy Somali businessman, reads a USA Today
as he eats. The driver approaches.

>   DRIVER
>   (subtitled)
>   Ready, Mr. Atto.

EXT. MOGADISHU MARKET - MOMENTS LATER

The driver leads Atto to the waiting car. Hoot watches,
speaks into a microphone in his collar.

>   HOOT
>   Leaving.

Atto gets in his car and leaves.

EXT. HIGH OVER NORTH MOGADISHU - DAY

Atto's caravan speeds through the dusty streets.

EXT. HIGH OVER THE DESERT - LATER

Several Black Hawk Helicopters track the caravan out of town.

INT. ATTO'S CAR

Atto smokes a cigar in the back seat, talks on his cell
phone. A Black Hawk Helicopter appears out the truck's
window, flying beside them.

>   DRIVER
>   (subtitled)
>   Sir!

Atto looks out the window at the Black Hawk.

>   ATTO
>   (subtitled)
>   Keep driving.

(CONTINUED)

CONTINUED:

A Ranger fires at the hood of Atto's car, spraying oil all
over the windshield.

An MH-6 Little Bird, a transport chopper with two outside
benches, lands in front of the caravan, forcing them to stop.
Rangers surround Atto's vehicle and tap on the glass.

                    ATTO (CONT'D)
             (calmly into phone, subtitled)
      I'm going to be late. Call you back.

INT. INTERROGATION ROOM

Silence. The room is dark, except for the dusty yellow
streaks cast from the window.

Atto sits at a table as GENERAL GARRISON enters and sets a
cup opposite him. Garrison wears khaki shorts and T-shirt
and dons sunglasses in the poorly lit room. He's laconic.
Steady.

Atto offers Garrison a cigar.

                    GARRISON
      No, no thanks. I've got one.

                    ATTO
      These are Cuban. Bolivar. Bellicoso.

Garrison holds up his own cigar.

                    GARRISON
             (unimpressed, simply)
      So's this.

                    ATTO
             (laughs)
      Miami, my friend, is not Cuba...

Garrison simply stares out the window. Atto lights his
cigar, regards it for a moment.

                    ATTO (CONT'D)
      I see not catching Aidid is becoming a
      routine.

                    GARRISON
      We weren't trying to catch Aidid, we were
      trying to catch you.

                    ATTO
    Me?
             (laughs)
              (MORE)

(CONTINUED)

CONTINUED:

                    ATTO (CONT'D)
          But am I that important? I hardly think
          so.

                    GARRISON
          You're just a business man.

                    ATTO
          Trying to make a living.

Garrison finally takes a seat opposite Atto.

                    GARRISON
          Selling guns to Aidid's militia.

                    ATTO
               (a beat, gravely)
          You've been here what, six weeks? Six
          weeks you are trying to catch the
          General. You put up your wanted posters.
          $25,000… what is this, gunfight at the
          K.O. corral?

                    GARRISON
               (laughs)
          It's ah, it's the O.K. Corral.

                    ATTO
          Do you think bringing me in will make him
          suddenly come to you? Make him more
          agreeable? Hmm?

                    GARRISON
               (simply)
          You know where he sleeps. You pay for
          his beds, much less his militia.
               (the bottom line)
          We're not leaving Somalia until we find
          him. And we will find him.

                    ATTO
               (immediately)
          Don't make the mistake of thinking
          because I grew up without running water
          I'm simple, General. I do know something
          about history. See all this? It's
          simply shaping tomorrow -- a tomorrow
          without a lot of Arkansas white-boy's
          ideas in it.

                    GARRISON
          Well, I wouldn't know about that, I'm
          from Texas.

                                        (CONTINUED)

> ATTO
> Mr. Garrison, I think you shouldn't have
> come here. This is civil war. This is
> our war, not yours.

> GARRISON
> (finally rips off his
> sunglasses)
> 300,000 dead and counting. That's not a
> war, Mr. Atto, that's genocide. Now you
> enjoy that tea, you hear?

Garrison exits swiftly past two U.S. Marine guards.

INT. HELICOPTER HANGAR - CONTINUOUS

Garrison strides through the hangar, past helicopters.

> GARRISON
> How'd he strike you?

JOE CRIBBS, a tall, lean man a few years younger than
Garrison, falls into step beside the General.

> CRIBBS
> Urbane, sophisticated. Cruel.

> GARRISON
> Yeah, he's a good catch.
> (they stop)
> It'll take some time, but Aidid'll feel
> the loss.

> CRIBBS
> I'm not sure time is something we've got
> in great supply.

> GARRISON
> This isn't Iraq, you know. It's more
> complicated than that.

Garrison starts away. Cribbs trails him.

> CRIBBS
> Boss, most of Washington might disagree.
> I'm just saying, they've been calling for
> these dang situation reports every
> morning this week.

> GARRISON
> (slips the sunglasses back on)
> Well, tell 'em the situation is ah,
> fragile.

CONTINUED:

And with that Garrison exits a door into BLINDING SUNLIGHT.

EXT. MOGADISHU AIPORT - DAY

SUPER: MOGADISHU AIRPORT

        U.S. ARMY HEADQUARTERS

INT. BLACK HAWK SUPER SIX ONE - DAY

Black Hawk pilot CLIFF "ELVIS" WOLCOTT addresses his Ranger
passengers as he prepares for take-off.

                    WOLCOTT
          Well ladies and gentlemen, my name is
          Cliff "Elvis" Wolcott. I'll be your
          pilot this afternoon. Federal
          regulations has designated this is a non-
          smoking Black Hawk helicopter. For those
          of you enrolled in our Mogadishu frequent
          flyer program, you'll be earning a
          hundred free credits this afternoon, and
          as always, the air sickness bags are
          located in the seat back in front of you.

                    BRILEY
          Number one indications are good, Cliff.

                    ELVIS
          You got it.

                    BRILEY
          Clear on two.

                    RANGER
          And you're still clear at one.

The Black Hawk takes off into the blaring sun.

INTERCUT BETWEEN BLACK HAWK SUPER SIX ONE AND DURANT'S BLACK
HAWK as they skirt the coastline.

                    DURANT
          Six One, this is Six Four. Go to UHF
          secure. I've got some bad news.

                    WOLCOTT
          Limo's a word Durant, I don't want to
          hear about it.

                    DURANT
          It is not a word, it's an abbreviation of
          a word.

                                        (CONTINUED)

CONTINUED:

                    WOLCOTT
          Limo is a word in common usage. That is
          the key phrase in Scrabble, my good
          friend. Common usage.

                    DURANT
          No! If it is not in the dictionary, it
          doesn't count.

                    WOLCOTT
          It doesn't have to be in the dictionary!

                    DURANT
          It does have to be in the dictionary!

                    WOLCOTT
          They don't say limousine, they say limo!

                    DURANT
          Listen, when we get back to the base,
          it's coming off the board.

Durant and Elvis rubber-neck as they pass each other, flying
opposite directions.

                    WOLCOTT
          You touch my limo and I'll spank you,
          night stalker, you hear me?

                    DURANT
          Yeah, promises.

                    OTHIC
          That's a nice beach down there. How's
          the water?

                    DURANT
          Yeah, it's nice and warm. It's loaded
          with sharks.

INT. OFFICE - DAY

The clean slap of computer keys. A cigarette smolders.
Ranger clerk SGT. JOHN GRIMES types data into a computer.
Standing opposite his desk is PFC TODD BLACKBURN.

                    GRIMES
          Name?

                    BLACKBURN
          Todd.

                                        (CONTINUED)

CONTINUED:

                    GRIMES
          Last name?

                    BLACKBURN
          Blackburn.

                    GRIMES
               (Grimes enters the info)
          First name Todd.

                    BLACKBURN
          So what's it like?

                    GRIMES
               (without looking up)
          What's what like?

                    BLACKBURN
          Mogadishu. The fighting.

                    GRIMES
          Serial number?

                    BLACKBURN
          7-2-1-6-3-4-2-7.

                    GRIMES
               (enters the info, then)
          Firstly, it's "The Mog," or simply:
          "Mog." No one calls it Mogadishu here.
          Secondly, I wouldn't know about the
          fighting, so don't ask.

                    BLACKBURN
          Why not?

                    GRIMES
          Didn't I just say "don't ask"?
               (takes a drag off cigarette)
          Look kid, you look like you're about
          twelve, so let me explain something to
          you. I have a rare and mysterious skill
          that precludes me from going on missions.

                    BLACKBURN
          Typing?

                    GRIMES
               (pauses typing)
          Can you type?

                    BLACKBURN
          No.

                                        (CONTINUED)

CONTINUED: (2)

                    GRIMES
              (immediately resumes typing)
         Date of birth?

                    BLACKBURN
         2-27-75.

Like chiseling into a headstone, Grimes types into the "age"
field — 18. Hands young Blackburn his I.D.

                    BLACKBURN (CONT'D)
              (affirmatively)
         Well I'm here to kick some ass.

EXT. DESERT COASTLINE - DAY

Hoot smokes a cigar on top of a sand dune as a Black Hawk
passes over him. We see that he is holding his mountain
bike.

Wolcott lands the Black Hawk Super Six One on the beach,
kicks up a storm of sand. Hoot shoulders his bike, hustles
into the chopper.

INT. BLACK HAWK SUPER SIX ONE - SAME

                    HOOT
              (over the ROAR of the chopper
              blades)
         Nice man, very smooth!

                    GORDON
              (impressed with himself)
         Single shot through the engine block!

                    HOOT
         Shit, that's a shame man. That's a nice
         jeep.

The Black Hawk lifts off and kicks up a cloud of sand as it
flies away.

EXT. BEACH FIRING RANGE - DAY

A line of Rangers fire M-16s at targets.

A military "Hummer" drives up to the range.

Behind the firing line, Eversmann blows a WHISTLE.

                                             (CONTINUED)

CONTINUED:

>   EVERSMANN
>   Cease fire, cease fire!
>   (the shooting stops)
>   Check your weapons.

Grimes and Blackburn approach from the Hummer.

>   GRIMES
>   Sergeant Eversmann!
>   (as Eversmann turns)
>   Sarge.

>   BLACKBURN
>   Private First Class Blackburn.

>   EVERSMANN
>   (blankly)
>   Yeah?

>   BLACKBURN
>   Reporting for duty.

>   EVERSMANN
>   Not to me you're not. You're reporting
>   to Lieutenant Beales. He should be
>   around here somewhere.

>   GRIMES
>   Can I leave him with you?

Grimes just wants to leave. He's got things to do.
Eversmann smirks -- go head, go.

>   EVERSMANN
>   Yeah, go ahead.
>   (to Blackburn)
>   You brought your weapon?

>   BLACKBURN
>   Sergeant. Want me to shoot? I'm rested.

>   EVERSMANN
>   When'd you get in?

>   BLACKBURN
>   Just now, Sergeant.

Blackburn looks so young and eager, and already sunburned
down one side of his face from the chopper ride.

EXT. HIGH ABOVE MARSHY WETLANDS - DAY

A herd of wild boars flees from the chopper.

INT. SUPER SIX ONE - SAME

Upon sight of the boars Hoot cocks his rifle.

>   HOOT
>   Hey, who's hungry?

The other Rangers smirk.

EXT. MESS HALL - EVENING

Hoot stands before a wild boar on a rotating BBQ spit. Men
move along the chow line.

CAPTAIN STEELE, Ranger ground commander, steps up behind
Delta Sergeant SANDERSON in line.

>   STEELE
>   What is this, Sanderson? Another
>   taxpayer funded Delta safari?

>   SANDERSON
>   Not if General Garrison's asking.

>   STEELE
>   No, I'm asking.

>   SANDERSON
>   Have a nice meal, Captain.

IN THE LINE -- Hoot cuts in front of Blackburn, grabs food.

>   BLACKBURN
>   Hey man, there's a line.

>   HOOT
>   I know.

>   BLACKBURN
>   Well, this isn't the back of it.

>   HOOT
>   Man, I know.

>   STEELE
>   Sergeant, Sergeant?

Hoot turns to see Steel staring at him.

>   STEELE (CONT'D)
>   What's going on here?

Sanderson watches them from down the chow line.

(CONTINUED)

CONTINUED:

          HOOT
Oh, just some aerial target practice sir,
didn't want to leave it behind.

          STEELE
I'm talking about your weapon. Delta or
no Delta, that's a hot weapon. You know
better than that. You're safety should
be on at all times on base.

          HOOT
    (shows Steele his finger)
Well this is my safety, sir.

Hoot walks off with his plate of food. Sanderson stops
Steele from going after Hoot.

          SANDERSON
Let it go sir, the guy hasn't eaten in a
couple of days.

          STEELE
You D-boys are a bunch of undisciplined
cowboys. Let me tell you something,
soldier. When we get on the five yard
line, you're gonna need my Rangers.
Ya'll better learn to be team players.
It's rough out there.

Sanderson walks away as LT. COLONEL MCKNIGHT watches from his
table.

INT. BARRACKS - NIGHT

The barracks is divided by the arrangement of the cots.
Rangers here, Delta there, relaxing over Risk, Stratego,
cribbage, cards, Gameboys. Ping-pong games in the corner.
Pilots Durant and Wolcott are continuing their Scrabble game.

PILLA stands before a group of young men as though he's on
stage. He imitates Captain Steele, much to the amusement of
the men. Pilla tries to hide his thick "Joyzee" accent:

          PILLA
Speak up!
    (touches his forehead)
You say this is your safety? Well this
is my boot son, and it will fit up your
ass with the proper amount of force.

Off to the side Eversmann writes a letter.

                                      (CONTINUED)

CONTINUED:

                         RANGER (OS)
          Is that a Jersey accent?

                         RANGER 2 (OS)
          It's Georgia.

                         PILLA
                    (to another Ranger)
          You'se guys, I'm trying to do this. Give
          me a break.
                    (back in character)
          Take those sunglasses off, Soldier.
          Delta wants to wear Oakleys, that's their
          business, I don't want to see them on you
          again, hooah?

Other Rangers laughingly mock his "hooah."

                         PILLA (CONT'D)
          Hey, is that a hot weapon?

DELTA SECTION - Gordon plops in a seat opposite Shughart as
Shughart studies a critical move, finger on his bishop.

                         GORDON
          Is that your move?

                         SHUGHART
          My hand on the piece?

                         GORDON
          I mate you in three whatever you do.

                         SHUGHART
          I'd keep my eye on that queen before
          counseling with others.

                         GORDON
          Well she's just lying in wait.

NEARBY - WEX, the oldest Delta at 42, sketches on a pad.
Busch leans over to see: a medieval knight dragging an
enormous sword through a dense forest. Beautiful and scary.

                         BUSCH
          Wex. It's good. You're improving.

                         WEX
                    (Wex shrugs, it's okay)
          Ah.

                         BUSCH
          If I may make a suggestion, observation?

                                             (CONTINUED)

CONTINUED: (2)

                        WEX
          Mmm hmm?

                        BUSCH
          It's a children's book, right?

                        WEX
          Right.

                        BUSCH
          They are not supposed to scare the living
          shit out of children.

                        WEX
          This is the part of the story where our
          knight, our warrior is about to slay the
          one-eyed dragon and that's scary.
          Besides, my daughter loves this stuff.

                        BUSCH
          I thought you finished that last week.
          Hmm?

                        WEX
          You done? I had to get a visual.

Across the hangar, Pilla is still doing his impression of
Steele for the group.

                        PILLA
          Hey, we are at the ten yard line here
          men, you understand? Can you count?
          One, two, ten. Okay? Where are my
          running backs? Where are my running
          backs?

The Rangers laugh and respond with emphatic "hooahs". Pilla
doesn't notice as Steele enters.

                        PILLA (CONT'D)
          Hey, I didn't see you in church on Sunday
          soldier. Had something more important to
          do? Not on Sunday you don't. Not
          anymore. I will make you believe. You
          understand?

Pilla turns and finds himself face-to-face with Steele
himself. Goes ashen. Other Rangers watch to see what
happens next. Steele, surprisingly, smiles good-naturedly.

                        STEELE
          That's pretty funny, hooah?

                                              (CONTINUED)

CONTINUED: (3)

The Rangers respond with a slight "hooah".

                  STEELE (CONT'D)
    See, it's a good impression. I recognize
    myself. All right, carry on.

Even though Steele seems to be taking it well, Pilla isn't
able to relax.

                  STEELE (CONT'D)
    A quick word, specials.

Pilla turns around and Steele grabs him in a headlock. The
Rangers laugh. Pilla flips the Rangers off behind his back.

                  PILLA
    Yes, Sir?

                  STEELE
    If I ever see you undermine me again,
    you'll be cleaning latrines with your
    tongue until you can't taste the
    difference between shit and french fries.
    Is that clear?

                  PILLA
    Hooah, sir.

                  STEELE
    All right.

The Rangers applaud Pilla as he returns and plops on a couch
between two guys.

ANOTHER CORNER - KURTH, WADDELL, NELSON, and GOODALE talk
around Eversmann, who busies himself with his letter. LT.
BEALES is reading a book on Somalia.

                  LT. BEALES
    Listen to this, if one skinny kills
    another skinny, his clan owes the dead
    guy's clan a hundred camels. A hundred
    camels.

Waddell looks up from his book.

                  WADDELL
    Camels. I wouldn't pay one camel.

                  GOODALE
    Must be a lot of fucking camel debt.
        (carves on a piece of wood)
    Is that really true lieutenant?

                              (CONTINUED)

CONTINUED: (4)

                    LT. BEALES
          Ask Sergeant Eversmann. He likes the
          skinnies.

Eversmann finally looks up.

                    GOODALE
          Eversmann, you really like the skinnies?

                    EVERSMANN
          It's not that I like them or I don't like
          them. I respect them.

Kurth leans back in his chair and deals the cards.

                    KURTH
          See, what you guys fail to realize is,
          Sergeant here is a bit of an idealist.
          Believes in this mission down to his very
          bones. Don't you, Sergeant?

                    EVERSMANN
          Look these people, they have no jobs, no
          food, no education, no future. I just
          figure that, you know, I mean, we either,
          we have two things we can do, we can
          either help, or we can sit back and
          watch the country destroy itself on CNN.
          Right?

                    KURTH
          I don't know about you guys, but I was
          trained to fight. Were you trained to
          fight, Sergeant?

They wait for an answer. Lt. Beales watches him with bemused
interest. Eversmann chooses his words carefully.

                    EVERSMANN
          Well, I think I was trained to make a
          difference, Kurth.

Kurth starts laughing.

                    LT. BEALES
          Like the man said, he's an idealist.
              (he looks at the TV)
          Oh wait, this is my favorite part.

ON SCREEN - A sniper fires at Steve Martin, who ducks for
cover in the gas station.

CONTINUED: (5)

Everyone cracks up, but no one as hard as Beales. Beales is literally falling off his chair. It takes a moment for the others to realize he isn't laughing; he's choking on his tongue, having a seizure.

A Ranger hurries to his side, waves the others back.

> RANGER
> No-no-no! Stay back, stay back!

Eversmann stands, moves closer for a better look. The Ranger cradles Beales.

> RANGER (CONT'D)
> John, John, it's okay. John, John, John, it's okay.

EXT. MOSQUE - MOGADISHU - DAWN

A speaker high atop a mosque calls out a morning prayer.

SUPER: 5:45 AM - SUNDAY, OCTOBER 3

EXT. BEACH - DAWN

A young Somali wearing a baseball cap backwards is on his knees, praying on the deserted beach in front of the old city. Then shoulders his rifle and gathers his things to go.

EXT. INFIRMARY — MORNING

Eversmann waits outside the tent as Steele approaches.

> STEELE
> Well, he'll be fine, but not in this army. He's out of the game. He's epileptic, going home.
> (walks past Eversmann, turns back)
> I'm putting you in charge of his chalk.
> (off Eversmann's reaction)
> You got a problem with that?

> EVERSMANN
> No, sir.

> STEELE
> Now it's a big responsibility. Your men are going to look to you to make the right decisions. Their lives depend on it.

CONTINUED:

That's great.   That makes Eversmann feel more anxious about
it.

                        STEELE (CONT'D)
          All right.

                        EVERSMANN
          Rangers are the way, Sir.

                        STEELE
          All the way.   Good luck, son.

Steele walks away.   Eversmann turns back to the Infirmary
tent, enters and waves to Beales, considering the enormity of
the duty he's just been given.

EXT. BAKARA MARKET - DAY

SUPER: HALWADIG ROAD - BAKARA MARKET

        AIDID'S MILITIA STRONGHOLD

Cacophony of noise and voices. The crowded outdoor Bakara
Market is in the center of the city.

The young baseball cap wearing Somali (TYE-DIE) we saw
praying on the beach now stands before a merchant who wants
to sell him a machine gun, demonstrating by firing into the
air. No one even looks over.

"Tie-Dye" appears to be more interested in a group of
militiamen talking above the stall's belts of ammunition, up
on the balcony.

A door opens behind them and two of Aidid's Lieutenants
emerge. The armed militiamen get up and escort the pair past
Tie-Dye without a look or word of acknowledgement except the
last of them, who gives the subtlest of gestures - an almost
imperceptible nod.

                        GARRISON (V.O.)
          A long-anticipated meeting of Aidid's
          senior cabinet may take place today at
          fifteen hundred hours.

INT. MESH TENT - DAY

Garrison briefs Delta, Black Hawk pilots, and four Ranger
chalk leaders, including Eversmann. McKnight, Steele, Cribbs,
Matthews and Harrell are in front, the rest behind.

                                              (CONTINUED)

CONTINUED:

                    GARRISON
          And I say may, because we all know by
          now, with the intel we get on the street,
          nothing is certain. This is actual
          intel, confirmed by three sources. Two
          tier one personalities may be present.
               (points to two enlarged photos)
          Omar Salad, Aidid's top political
          advisor; and Abdi Hassan Awale, interior
          minister. These are the guys we're
          after.

Delta let the photos burn into their retinas. Garrison looks
at Captain Steele.

                    GARRISON (CONT'D)
          Today we go. Same mission template as
          before.

Garrison's hand moves past an overhead map of Mogadishu,
points to another map: the outline of a general "target
building." Two building entrances are marked "D" for Delta.
The men take notes as they listen.

                    GARRISON (CONT'D)
          15:45, Assault Force Delta will
          infiltrate the target building and seize
          all suspects within. Security Force:
          Rangers. Four Ranger chalks under the
          command of Captain Steele will rope in at
          15:46...
               (points to four corners on map)
          ...and hold a four-corner perimeter around
          the target building. No one gets in or
          out.
               (as McKnight looks on)
          Extraction Force: Lt. Colonel McKnight's
          Humvee column will drive into the city at
          15:47 on Halwadig Road and hold just
          short of the Olympic Hotel, here --
               (points to the map)
          Wait for the green light. Now once Delta
          gives the word, McKnight's column will
          move to the target building and load the
          prisoners on flatbed trucks. Immediately
          after the prisoners are loaded, the four
          Ranger Chalks will collapse back to the
          target building, load up on Humvees, and
          the entire ground force will exfil the
          three miles back to base. Mission time
          from incursion to extraction: no longer
          than 30 minutes.

                                        (CONTINUED)

CONTINUED: (2)

Garrison, still standing before them, lets this sink in.

                    GARRISON (CONT'D)
          Now, I had requested light armor and AC-
          130 Spectre Gunships, but Washington, in
          all it's wisdom, decided against this.
          Too high-profile. Black Hawks and Little
          Birds will provide the air cover with
          miniguns and 275 rockets. Colonel
          Harrell?

Garrison sits as he glances over at COLONEL HARRELL.

                    HARRELL
          In the C 2 Bird: Colonel Matthews will
          coordinate the air mission, and I will
          coordinate ground forces.
          Colonel Matthews?

COLONEL MATTHEWS, early forties, speaks up.

                    MATTHEWS
          Mission launch codeword is Irene.
          Questions?

                    HOOT
          Which building is it, sir?

                    GARRISON
          Exactly which building we're confirming
          right now. Somewhere around the Bakara
          Market.

Garrison regards Hoot's reaction, then the others.

                    GARRISON (CONT'D)
               (primarily to Hoot)
          I don't choose the time or place of their
          meetings.

                    HOOT
          I didn't say a word, Sir.

There is an unspoken unease in the room.

                    GARRISON
          We're going into the hornet's nest today.
          You give them time to react and they'll
          swarm. Make no mistake. Once you're in
          the Bakara Market, you're in an entirely
          hostile district. Don't underestimate
          their capabilities.

                                        (CONTINUED)

CONTINUED: (3)

Eversmann swallows, checks the others' reactions.

                    GARRISON (CONT'D)
          Now we'll be going through friendly
          neighborhoods before we hit the market.
          So remember the "Rules of Engagement": no
          one fires unless fired upon. So let's go
          get this thing done. Good luck,
          gentlemen.

EXT. TENT - MOMENTS LATER

The group files out. McKnight, the most obviously concerned
of them, lights a cigarette and slaps closed his Zippo
lighter. Eversmann watches from inside the tent as Colonels
Matthews and Harrell walk up to McKnight.

                    MATTHEWS
          What's the matter, Danny, something you
          don't like?

                    MCKNIGHT
              (as if it's nothing)
          No Spectre gunships, daylight instead of
          night, late afternoon when they're all
          fucked up on khat, only part of the city
          Aidid can mount a serious counter-attack
          on short notice, what's not to like?

                    HARRELL
          Life's imperfect.

                    MCKNIGHT
          Yeah, for you two, circling above it at
          500 feet, it's imperfect. Down in the
          street, it's unforgiving.

Eversmann continues to watch from inside the tent. He heard
it all.

EXT. MOGADISHU - DAY

An alley. Tie-Dye rips lengths of black duct tape and
presses them to the roof of his battered car in the shape of
an X.

EXT. BASE - DAY

Smith plays basketball as Eversmann works at a desk.

                    EVERSMANN
          What the fuck, Smith?

                                              (CONTINUED)

CONTINUED:

                    SMITH
          Well?

                    EVERSMANN
          Well, what?

                    SMITH
          We going?

                    EVERSMANN
          Why should I tell you that?

                    SMITH
          Because I'm me.

                    EVERSMANN
          Three o'clock. Downtown. Bakara market.

                    SMITH
          Alright.

                    EVERSMANN
          Listen, Smith. I need you to back me up
          out there today, all right? Keep sharp.

                    SMITH
          Yes sir, Sergeant Eversmann.

                    EVERSMANN
          All right.

                    SMITH
          Ev?
               (hot-dogs with the basketball)
          It's gonna be nothing man. Nothing.

Smith runs off in to the hangar bouncing the basketball.

INT. BASE OFFICE — DAY

At a filing cabinet, Grimes carefully pushes the plunger down
on the coffee grounds in the coffee pot. He speaks over his
shoulder to the only other person in the cluttered office —
Sizemore.

                    GRIMES
          It's all in the grind, Sizemore. Can't
          be too fine, can't be too coarse. This
          my friend is a science.

Turns, holding the coffee pot.

                                                      (CONTINUED)

CONTINUED:

                    GRIMES (CONT'D)
          I mean - you're looking at the guy that
          believed the commercials, you know?
          About be all you can be. I made coffee
          through Desert Storm. I made coffee
          through Panama, while everyone else got
          to fight, got to be a Ranger.

As Grimes blathers, Sizemore reaches for a letter opener,
shoves it down his still-drying cast and scratches away.

                    GRIMES (CONT'D)
          Now it's Grimesy, black, one sugar. Or
          Grimesy, got a powdered anywhere?

Adds just the right amount of sugars. Grimes finally turns
and approaches Sizemore, sitting at a desk, trying to itch
under the still-wet cast. Hands Sizemore the mug.

                    GRIMES (CONT'D)
          What happened to you?

                    SIZEMORE
          Ping—pong accident.

                    GRIMES
          What?

                    SIZEMORE
          So guess what? Your wish has been
          granted. You're going out today.

                    GRIMES
          You're fuckin' me.

                    SIZEMORE
          You're taking my place assisting the
          sixty gunner. Sergeant Eversmann said to
          get your stuff and get ready.

Now Grimes is speechless. Sizemore relishes the moment.

                    SIZEMORE (CONT'D)
          It's what you wanted, isn't it?

                    GRIMES
               (gripping his coffee)
          Oh yeah. Hell, yeah.

Grimes is apoplectic. His eyes glaze over with a thousand-
yard stare. It's exactly what he wanted, but now that it's
come to him, he's not at all sure it's what he really wants.

INT. HANGAR - DAY

Delta and Rangers, in their respective areas, prepare in
their own ways, gathering equipment they think they'll need,
leaving behind what they don't.

Eversmann calls out to Grimes.

                    EVERSMANN
          Grimsey! I want you to stick with
          Waddell and give him ammo when he needs
          it. Hooah?

                    GRIMES
               (softly)
          Hooah.

                    WADDELL
          I wouldn't worry 'bout that. Generally
          speaking, Somalis can't shoot for shit.

                    GALENTINE
          Don't worry about it. Just watch out for
          the Sammies throwing the fucking rocks
          and you'll be fine. Might even be fun.

The other guys snicker at this.

                    KURTH
          You boys do their thing now. What we
          gotta do is cover them, choppers gonna
          cover us. And we'll be all right.

                    EVERSMANN
          Look you guys, I know this is my first
          time as ah, Chalk leader...but ah, this
          is serious. We're Rangers, not some
          sorry ass J.R.O.T.C. We're elite. Let's
          act like it out there. Hooah?

The guys all "hooah".

                    EVERSMANN (CONT'D)
          Any questions? We're gonna be okay. All
          right, grab your gear. Let's move out.

A few guys "hooah" again, disperse. Eversmann exhales
heavily.

INTERCUT, Delta, methodical and precise, no talk: Hoot
taping the pins of grenades. Grimes starts to fill a
canteen.

                                        (CONTINUED)

CONTINUED:

                    NELSON
          You're not going to need that, dude,
          we're not out there long enough.

Grimes sets it back. Sees YUREK reach for a NOD - Night
Observation Device - and reaches for one himself.

                    TWOMBLY
          Hey, you're not going to need that
          either, we're back before dark. You
          might as well take dope and beer instead.

Grimes just stares. Twombly, of course, is kidding.

                    GRIMES
          What?

                    TWOMBLY
          Ammo, dude. Take ammo.

Yurek puts the NODs back. Grimes sees Joyce removing the
rear panel of his Kevlar vest. Joyce notices Grimes
watching.

                    JOYCE
          Let me tell you something Grimes. You've
          got about fifty pounds of gear as it is,
          you don't need another twelve. I don't
          know about you but, I'm not planning on
          getting shot in the back running away.

                    GRIMES
          Well I better keep mine in.

                    EVERSMANN
          Hey, Grimes? The most important thing?
          Just remember when everybody else is
          shooting, shoot in the same direction.
          All right.

INTERCUT: Eversmann considers Blackburn, who appears more
fidgety than before.

As Joyce's putting on his armor, he watches Wex across the
hangar tearing off pieces of masking tape and writing
something on them with a Sharpie. Sticks them to his boots.

                    JOYCE
          Look at this guy, Lo. Taping his blood
          type to his boots. It's bad luck.

                    RUIZ
          No it's smart.

                                              (CONTINUED)

CONTINUED: (2)

SGT. LORENZO RUIZ pulls out an already addressed and sealed
envelope, regards it.

                    RUIZ (CONT'D)
          All Delta do that.

                    JOYCE
                (re: the letter)
          That's bad luck too, man. Come on, let's
          go.

Ruiz holds the letter. Joyce gets up and walks past him.
Ruiz turns to a glum Sizemore.

                    RUIZ
          It's a good thing you're right handed,
          Adonis.
                (mimes like he's jacking off)
          If not, I don't know what you'd do.

                    SIZEMORE
          You're a funny guy, man.

Ruiz profers the letter to Sizemore.

                    SIZEMORE (CONT'D)
          I'm not taking no death letter.

                    RUIZ
                (shoves it in his hand)
          We have a deal.

                    SIZEMORE
          I'll give it back to you in an hour.

INT. BARRACKS — CONTINUED - DAY

                    EVERSMANN
          You okay?

                    BLACKBURN
          Excited. In a good way. I've been
          training my whole life for this.

                    EVERSMANN
          You ever shot at anybody before?

                    BLACKBURN
          No, Sargent.

CONTINUED:

                              EVERSMANN
                    Me neither.

Eversmann pats Blackburn on the shoulder.

EXT. MOGADISHU - DAY

SUPER: 2:29 PM

A Black Hawk hovers over Tie-Dye's battered car.

INT. TIE-DYE'S CAR MOVING - DAY

Tie-Dye drives along the streets, deeper into the city than
the U.N. ever goes.

EXT. HIGH ABOVE MOGADISHU - SAME

A Black Hawk hovers high above the car, following.

INT. JOC - SAME

SUPER: J.O.C. JOINT OPERATIONS CENTER

Garrison and Cribbs watch the image from the C2 chopper, and
HEAR the annoying music over the command net.

                              CRIBBS
                    Think he's reliable?

                              GARRISON
                    Well, we'll see. It's his first time
                    out.

INT. TIE-DYE'S CAR MOVING - DAY

Local pop music jangles on the radio as Tie-Dye drives. He
drips with sweat.

INT. JOC - SAME

                              GARRISON
                    Tell him to turn his damn radio off.

                              RADIOMAN (OS)
                    Yes, sir. Tell him to turn his radio
                    off.

INT. BLACK HAWK HELICOPTER - SAME

                              HARRELL
                    Abdu, you need to turn your radio off.

INT. TIE-DYE'S CAR MOVING - DAY

Tie-Dye follows the order, switches the radio off.

INT. KITCHEN — U.S./TIME DIFFERENCE - DAY

The machine sitting on a counter next to a refrigerator
covered with snapshots and reminder notes. A dog listens to
the outgoing message:

> CHILD'S VOICE (V.O.)
> Hi, mommy and daddy aren't home. Leave
> me a message.

> SHUGHART (V.O.)
> Hey baby, it's me, you there? Pick up if
> you're there.

INT. THE HANGAR - DAY

Shughart is on a satellite phone, huddled against a wall.

> SHUGHART (CONT'D)
> I'm just calling to check up on you and
> make sure everything's all right. I'll
> call in a couple of hours. You better
> not be sleeping.

Gordon moves a chess piece, then passes Shughart still on the
phone.

> GORDON
> You're move, Randy.

INT. KITCHEN — U.S./TIME DIFFERENCE - NIGHT

> SHUGHART
> I'm missing you. I love you, baby.

The call disconnects.

> SHUGHART'S WIFE
> Hello, hello?

EXT. BARRACKS BUILDING - DAY

Eversmann leans against a wall next to Hoot. Silence between
them, Eversmann looks off.

> EVERSMANN
> You know, it's kinda funny. Beautiful
> beach, beautiful sun...it'd almost be a
> good place to visit.

(CONTINUED)

CONTINUED:

                      HOOT
Almost.

                      EVERSMANN
          (off Hoot's tone)
You don't think we should be here.

                      HOOT
Know what I think? Don't really matter
what I think. Once that first bullet
goes past your head — politics, and all
that shit -- just goes right out the
window.

                      EVERSMANN
I just wanna do it right today.

                      HOOT
Just watch your corner...get all your men
back here alive.

Eversmann turns to Hoot, grave.

EXT. MOGADISHU - DAY

Tie-Dye's car moves deeper into the city.

INT. JOC - SAME

An overhead image of Tie-Dye's car and surrounding streets.

                      GARRISON
Is this supposed to be the place or did
his car just take a dump?

                OBSERVATION BIRD PILOT (O.S.)
Avi come in.

INT. OBSERVATION BIRD

                  OBSERVATION BIRD PILOT
Avi, can you hear me? Is this the place?

INT. TIE-DYE'S CAR

Tie-Dye sits and stares at the people in the street.

                OBSERVATION BIRD PILOT (V.O.)
Avi, come in? Avi, can you hear me, is
this the place?

                    TIE-DYE
To my right hand side, above the cafe.

INT. JOC - SAME

                    MATTHEWS
          Sir, he says this is the building.

                    CRIBBS
          He's certain?

Garrison looks at the overhead images.

INT. OBSERVATION BIRD - CONTINUED

                    OBSERVATION BIRD PILOT (V.O.)
          Avi, you need to be sure. Are you sure?

INT. TIE-DYE'S CAR - CONTINUED

                    TIE-DYE
          Well, it's down the road two blocks
          around my left.

INT./EXT. OBSERVATION BIRD - CONTINUED

                    OBSERVATION BIRD PILOT (V.O.)
          Now he's saying the building's actually a
          couple blocks down, but if he's seen
          outside it he'll be shot.

INT. JOC — CONTINUED

                    GARRISON
          I'll fuckin' shoot him myself a couple of
          blocks down. Tell him I want his skinny
          ass parked in front of the damn building.
          He's not getting paid until he does
          exactly that.

EXT. BASE - DAY

McKnight addresses his men.

                    MCKNIGHT
          It's three miles to the target area.
          We're never off the main roads.

In the background, soldiers move and prepare MH—6 Little
Birds.

                    MCKNIGHT (CONT'D)
          At the K—4 traffic circle we turn north,
          then east on National. We wait 'til
          Delta's finished, here. Then we roll up
          in force on Halwadig.
                    (MORE)

                                        (CONTINUED)

CONTINUED:

>   MCKNIGHT (CONT'D)
>   We load the prisoners and then the
>   assault and blocking forces, and bring
>   'em back. Home in an hour. Okay?

McKnight looks at Pilla, Othic, other gunners.

>   MCKNIGHT (CONT'D)
>   Now there will be some shooting. Bakara
>   Market is the Wild West. But be careful
>   what you shoot at because people do live
>   there. Hooah.

Several "hooah" in response as McKnight and the rest up and
leave.

EXT. MOGADISHU - DAY

Tie-Dye's car moves through the streets.

INT. JOC - CONTINUED - DAY

The overhead image of Tie-Dye's car on a screen.

>   GARRISON
>   The last one of these guys shot himself
>   in the head playing Russian Roulette in a
>   bar.

EXT. HALWADIG ROAD - DAY

Tie-Dye's car rattles up to a three-story building. Stops.

INT. JOC - CONTINUED

The overhead image on a screen.

>   RADIOMAN (OS)
>   Sir, the vehicle stopped.

>   GARRISON
>   So this is the real deal now? He's sure
>   this time?

>   OBSERVATION BIRD PILOT (V.O.)
>   He sounds scared shitless.

>   GARRISON
>   Good. That's always a good sign.

EXT. HALWADIG ROAD - CONTINUED

Tie-Dye exits the car, opens the hood. Fans the steaming
radiator fumes.

INT. JOC - CONTINUED

The overhead image on a screen.

> GARRISON
> (turning to leave)
> Alright, all QRF out of the airspace.

> CRIBBS
> All QRF out of the airspace.

INT. MATTHEW'S C2 BLACK HAWK - DAY

Colonel Matthews speaks into his headset:

> MATTHEWS
> All units, Irene. I say again, Irene.

INT. WOLCOTT'S BLACK HAWK - CONT.

Wolcott and his copilot make sure things are in order.

> WOLCOTT
> (into his headset)
> Irene!

INT. DURANT'S BLACK HAWK - DAY

Durant smiles, speaks into his headset.

> DURANT
> Fuckin' Irene!

EXT. TARMAC - DAY

Rangers deploy across the tarmac to their respective choppers.

Garrison has come out to wish the men well, moving past the open doors of Eversmann's Black Hawk, shouting over the noise.

> GARRISON
> Good luck boys...be careful...no one gets
> left behind.

He gives the thumbs up and leaves. Blackburn and Grimes notice Eversmann still looking after the general with some concern.

> BLACKBURN & GRIMES
> (almost together)
> What's wrong?

(CONTINUED)

CONTINUED:

                    EVERSMANN
          Nothing. He's just never done that
          before.

                    GRIMES
          Ah, fuck!

GETTING INTO A TRUCK - MCKNIGHT

                    MCKNIGHT
          Let's go!

McKnight's Humvee column rumbles away from the tarmac.

IN SUPER SIX ONE — Elvis Wolcott flashes a satisfied grin at
the sound of the code word. He lifts tip on the controls as -
- THE ARMADA ascends, deafening. Little Birds whirl skyward,
Delta carried aloft outside the choppers, the ultimate thrill
ride. Black Hawks rise from the earth in tight formation.

INT. PRISON ROOM — SAME TIME - DAY

The dark, barely-furnished room from before. Alone in it,
Atto watches a glass rattle across the table from the thunder
of the helicopters taking off outside.

EXT. SOMALIA COAST NEAR BASE - DAY

Just outside the base, against barren terrain near the coast,
a kid wearing a BeeGees t-shirt and flip—flops tends a small
fire.

As the helicopters continue to rise, the boy finds a cell
phone in his pants pocket and makes a call.

EXT. ROOFTOP/STREET - MOGADISHU - DAY

Another kid with a cell phone hurries across a rooftop. He
shouts down --

                    SOMALI KID
          Mo'Alim!

The kid drops the phone. It falls into a waiting pair of
hands of an Aidid militia man. He carries the phone in to
MO'ALIM, an Aidid lieutenant, sprawled out asleep on a bed.

                    MILITIA MAN
          Mo'Alim!

The Militia Man wakes Mo'Alim up with the phone. Mo'Alim
puts the phone to his ear and hears a Doppler-thunder of
helicopters --

EXT. SOMALIA COAST BY EAST - CONTINUED - DAY

The first boy is holding the phone up like a badge as the helicopters thunder over him.

INT. MARKET - DAY

Mo'Alim and his militia arm themselves. Men shout and pass off guns to more men.

INT./EXT. WOLCOTT'S BLACK HAWK / MOGADISHU - DAY

Black Hawks move low and fast, following the Humvee caravan along a road. Then parallel to the shore over the running breakers.

INT. WOLCOTT'S BLACK HAWK - CONT.

> EVERSMANN
> Grimsey!

Eversmann taps his helmet and throws a pen to Grimes. Grimes writes his name on his helmet.

> WOLCOTT
> Two minutes!

Eversmann holds up two fingers.

> EVERSMANN
> Two minutes.

EXT. MOGADISHU STREETS - DAY

Tie-Dye stands waiting outside his car.

The militia barricade the streets and start burning tires. Mo'Alim rides forward on a convoy.

INT. WOLCOTT'S BLACK HAWK - CONT.

BELOW — black smoke from piles of burning tires rises into the sky as--

> GRIMES
> (shouts in Nelson's ear)
> Why are they burning tires?

> WADDELL
> Signals, to the militia!

INT. JOC - CONT.

Garrison watches the overhead image.

INT. WOLCOTT'S BLACK HAWK - CONTINUED

Briley holds up one finger and mouths one minute.

>   WOLCOTT
>   One minute.

>   EVERSMANN
>   One minute!

Waddell dog-ears a page of his book. Eversmann's chalk
prepares to go in.

Blackburn sees Nelson putting in a football mouth guard.

>   BLACKBURN
>   What's that for?

>   NELSON
>   Last rope, I almost bit my tongue off!

Nelson smiles back at him, black plastic over his teeth.

EXT. MOGADISHU STREETS - DAY

The Humvee convoy rolls in as people run through the streets.

EXT./INT. CAR - HALWADIG ROAD - DAY

Tie-Dye sits in his car and waits for the Black Hawks to
land. Militia run through the streets, firing sporadically.

SUPER: 3:42 PM

Little Birds land in the street. One of the Little Birds
streaks in and lands on the roof of the building. Hoot's and
the other two descend lower, onto the street, the rotors just
missing the walls of the building. A dust cloud envelopes
them all. Rangers deploy on the street and the Little Birds
swiftly take off.

Rangers move low and fast, storm into buildings in tactical
formations. Fire and kill militiamen.

Tie-Dye pulls away as a Black Hawk approaches the building
through the smoke. Ropes drop from some helicopters.

INT. WOLCOTT'S BLACK HAWK - DAY

Through the cockpit, Eversmann sees nothing below but a
massive swirling cloud of dust. Speaks into his headset mic:

> EVERSMANN
> Ropes!

FAST ROPES are kicked out the chopper door, snaking down into
the dust cloud as Eversmann's men prepare to go in. He
SHOUTS:

> EVERSMANN (CONT'D)
> GO! GO! GO!

Kurth, Goodale, Doc Schmid all start roping down. Bullets
are already PINGING off the belly of the Black Hawk.

INT. JOC - SAME

Garrison watches the overhead image.

INT./EXT. — TARGET BUILDING - DAY

Delta come through the dust and smoke of flashbangs like
apparitions. Hoot, Wex and other Delta burst into a room,
see ten Somalia trying to find another escape route. Better
dressed than most Somalis, this group carries file folders,
maps, charts, scattered on a table, and AK-47s. Bingo.

> HOOT
> Down, get down! DOWN! DOWN! DO IT NOW!
> NOW! NOW!

Somalis hit the deck, foot in the back for their troubles if
they don't do it fast enough. Surrendered weapons clatter to
the floor.

ON THE STREET

McKnight, now out of his Humvee, peeks calmly around the
corner of a building.

INT. WOLCOTT'S BLACK HAWK - DAY

Speaks into his headset mic:

> EVERSMANN
> Let's go, let's go!

The remaining men start roping down. Grimes swallows hard.
He's next. Crew Chief DOWDY shouts to him:

(CONTINUED)

CONTINUED:

                         DOWDY
              No fear!

                         GRIMES
              Oh yeah, right.

With that, Grimes disappears; down the rope sliding into the
dust and into the gunfire.

EXT. HALWADIG ROAD - DAY

McKnight's convoy reaches its waiting position just off
Halwadig. Pilla, in his turret, hears shots, sees bullets
spark off the side of the Humvee.

                         PILLA
              Colonel, they're shooting at us!
              Colonel, they're shooting at us!

                         MCKNIGHT
              Well shoot back!

A hail of gunfire erupts and Pilla swings the fifty turret.
Sights a technical racing toward him. He FIRES on it.

                         OBSERVATION BIRD PILOT (V.O.)
              Super Six Five leaving, going in to
              holding pattern.

                         OBSERVATION BIRD PILOT 2
              Super Six Two, come in. Take up
              perimeter pattern

                         OBSERVATION BIRD PILOT
              Roger that.

IN THE CHOPPER — still in silence, Blackburn remains.

                         EVERSMANN
              Go Blackburn, go! Go Blackburn!

Just as he says this, Eversmann sees an RPG streaking up at
them.

                         EVERSMANN (CONT'D)
                   (to Pilot)
              RPG!
                   (to Blackburn)
              Hold on!

The Black Hawk ROCKS to avoid the rocket.

                                              (CONTINUED)

CONTINUED:

--BLACKBURN reaches for the rope, sees it swing away and out of the grasp of his gloved hands, EVERSMANN stares as the kid FREE FALLS, disappearing into the swirling dust cloud.

Horrified, Eversmann dives out after him, grabbing onto the rope.

                    EVERSMANN (CONT'D)
          No!

EXT. CHALK 4 CORNER - SAME

Eversmann fast-ropes through the cloud for what seems to him forever. Finally, his feet touch down. He scrambles to Blackburn -- having fallen 40 feet to the dirt street.

                    OBSERVATION BIRD PILOT
          D-2, we got a man fallen.

                    OPERATOR
          Six Four, you're a sitting duck there.
          Get out and take cover pattern.

                    OBSERVATION BIRD PILOT
          Roger that. Six one leaving.

The Black Hawk starts away.

ON THE GROUND

Eversmann checks Blackburn who lies still. He and Blackburn are alone in the middle of the street. Over the sharp crackle of gunfire --

                    EVERSMANN
          Doc! Doc Schmid!

Schmid, the medic who benched Sizemore, suddenly appears with his kit from behind Eversmann, startling him.

                    SCHMID
          Where's he hit?

                    EVERSMANN
          He's not. He fell.

                    SCHMID
          What?

                    EVERSMANN
          He fell!

EXT. CHALK 4 CORNER - DAY

Grimes dives on his belly, bullets hissing through the air
around him. Waddell is sighting with the SAW, but not firing
at a group of fleeting figures down the block.

                    GRIMES
          Why aren't you shooting?

                    WADDELL
          We're not being shot at yet.

                    GRIMES
          How can you tell?

                    WADDELL
          A hiss means it's close. A snap...

SNAP!SNAP!SNAP!

                    WADDELL
          Now they're shooting at us!

Waddell levels withering fire down the street. The fleeting
figures scatter.

Grimes sees figures with weapons firing at him a block away.
He levels his gun and SHOOTS! He's shooting at the enemy!

EXT. CHALK 4 CORNER - DAY

Eversmann, in the middle of it with Blackburn, yells across
to his radio man, Galentine. Waves him over.

                    EVERSMANN
          Galentine! Get me Captain Steele! Get
          me Captain Steele!

                    GALENTINE
          Uniform Six Four, this is Uniform Two
          Five, come in, over. Uniform Six Five,
          this is Uniform Two Five Two.

Schmid moves Blackburn's head -- blood seeping from his nose
and ears.

                    GALENTINE (CONT'D)
          I can't get him!

Galentine doesn't know why. Something wrong with the radio
maybe. Eversmann unholsters his walkie-talkie, and as he
shouts into it, he can SEE Delta spilling from the first
building out into the street.

                                        (CONTINUED)

CONTINUED:

                    EVERSMANN
          Juliet Six Four, this is Chalk Four. We
          got a man down! We gotta get him out of
          here. Over!

EXT. INTERCUT - STEELE'S CHALK ONE - CONT.

Steele's men are fanned cut, taking random gunfire. Steele
sees the Delta, running down the block toward him and into a
different building. Eversmann's voice squawks on the walkie.

                    STEELE
          Six four, say again, two five, over!

                    EVERSMANN (V.O.)
          He's hurt. He fell. Over.

                    STEELE
          Take a breath Two Five and calm down!
          Over!

                    EVERSMANN
          Man down!

                    STEELE
          Missed your last response, again?

INT. JOC - SAME

Garrison sits down and watches the overhead image. He rubs
his temples.

EXT. CHALK 4 CORNER - SAME

Schmid shouts out to anyone.

                    SCHMID
          Get me a stretcher!

Two men unfold a collapsible litter from a medic pack. They
gingerly place Blackburn on it.

                    EVERSMANN
          Go!

                    SCHMID
          Okay, go!

They run through a hail of gun fire.

INT. TARGET BUILDING - DAY

Delta has moved the prisoners out on to the balcony. They kneel facing the wall.

                    HOOT
          Secure.

                    SANDERSON
          Let's move out!

                    HOOT
          Let's go, let's go!

EXT. HALWADIG ROAD

Schmid and his team carry Blackburn on the stretcher.

INT. TARGET BUILDING - DAY

Delta has marched the prisoners into an inner courtyard. Everyone waiting.

Hoot speaks into a walkie talkie --

                    HOOT
          K.O. Six Four, green light.

INT. JOC - DAY

Garrison sits at the panel of screens.

                    OBSERVATION BIRD PILOT (V.O.)
          Ready for extraction, over.

                    GARRISON
          That's it. We're done.

                    OBSERVATION BIRD PILOT 2 (V.O.)
          Roger that Kilo One One, we'll relay.
          Uniform Six Four, ready for extraction.

EXT. HALWADIG ROAD/HUMVEE SQUAD - DAY

McKnight shouts as he leaps into the Humvee:

                    MCKNIGHT
          Roger that. There's the call! Let's
          move out! Let's move out!

                    STRUECKER
          Hold on!

                                        (CONTINUED)

CONTINUED:

The Humvee squad rumbles around the corner, rolls down the line.

McKnight leads them to a Humvee, starts passing Blackburn inside to a waiting Delta medic.

EXT. HALWADIG ROAD - CONT.

Gunfire from rooftops across the street force Delta to bring out prisoners in contained groups of three. Other Delta return fire, driving back snipers. As soon as one disappears, another sniper pops up.

                    MCKNIGHT
          How much time do you need?

                    SANDERSON
          Five minutes, Sir!

                    MCKNIGHT
          What?

                    SANDERSON
          Five minutes!

                    MCKNIGHT
          You've only got five minutes!

McKnight turns around and walks over to Schmid.

                    MCKNIGHT (CONT'D)
          What happened to him?

                    SCHMID
          He fell, missed the rope.

                    MCKNIGHT
          How'd he do that?
             (off Schmid's shrug)
          Put him in that op!

Hoot comes back out of the target courtyard with Sanderson. They move the Somali prisoners out.

                    HOOT
          Let's go, let's go. Come on, let's move!

Blackburn is loaded in to a Humvee.

GRIMES has been engrossed in watching them load prisoners.

CONTINUED:

When he turns around be sees Schmid, Smith and Waddell WAY
THE HELL up the street, running back toward Chalk 4. He can
see them taking fire as they run, moving from cover to cover.

ON GRIMES - oh shit. He starts charging after them. Barely
gets three feet when a rocket explodes near him, causing him
to tumble. Turns and charges back to Chalk One and safety.

EXT. CHALK 4 CORNER - DAY

Schmid, Smith and Waddell come charging up, take cover, out
of breath from the long, dangerous run.

The rest of the chalk are spread out, returning fire.

Eversmann hears an approaching Little Bird and glances up.

As it thunders over him, hot casings splash down like rain,
burning him.

                    EVERSMANN
          Oh, fuck!

Eversmann pulls a casing out of his flack jacket.

INT. TARGET BUILDING - DAY

Hoot marches more prisoners out.

Two Somali boys stare at them from the corner like they're a
circus attraction.

                    HOOT
          Let's go, right here! Come on!

                    MCKNIGHT
               (calls out)
          Struecker!
               (grabs a radio)
          Formula C-4, I need to send out a three
          Humvee with a critical casualty, he looks
          real bad. I need to evac now!

INT. BLACK HAWK - SAME

                    HARRELL
          Roger that, Uniform Six Four. We'll shot
          a team of gunships to you, over.

INT. TARGET BUILDING - CONT.

                    MCKNIGHT
          Roger that.

                                        (CONTINUED)

CONTINUED:

McKnight grabs Sanderson.

                    MCKNIGHT (CONT'D)
          I need extra security on these Humvees.

Hoot motions for his team. Says to McKnight:

                    HOOT
          I'll go! I'll take my team, make sure
          they get back okay.

                    SANDERSON
              (nods)
          Sure.

                    MCKNIGHT
          Struecker, you're lead Humvee!

SERGEANT STRUECKER, Iowa farm boy, born-again Christian and
model Ranger jumps up.

                    STRUECKER
              Hooah!

EXT. TARGET BUILDING - CONT.

Strueker is behind the wheel of a Humvee, Blackburn in back,
Medic tending to him. Hoot and his team jumps in the
Humvees, Hoot riding shotgun next to Struecker.

Struecker hits the gas. The three Humvees take off.

INT/EXT. THE STRUECKER/BLACKBURN CONVOY - DAY

Snipers on the rooftops fire. A hail of shots hits the
trucks like a cadence of drums.

From the Humvees the turret men return fire. Pilla blasts
away with his .50, covering their asses.

                    MCKNIGHT
          How're things going? Are things okay
          there, Struecker?

                    STRUECKER
          I don't want to talk about it now,
          Colonel.

                    MCKNIGHT
          Anyone hit?

CONTINUED:

Struecker and Hoot see a roadblock. Turns onto another street
to avoid it - two other Humvees following - and finds himself
in a killing zone. Complete chaos.

In the turret, Pilla continues to fire. On the street, a
Militia Man spin out from behind a corner and shoots Pilla in
the head.

Suddenly the view swings straight up as he's hit in the head,
flops down into the Humvee, onto a stunned Ranger - Thomas.

Struecker turns in his seat, sees Pilla bleeding on Thomas,
who is hysterical.

                    THOMAS
          Christ, he's fucked up!

                    HOOT
          He's dead.

CUT BETWEEN CITY CENTER AND HUMVEE

                    MCKNIGHT
               (into radio)
          Struecker, talk to me!

                    STRUECKER
               (long pause, then)
          It's Sergeant Pilla.

                    MCKNIGHT
          What's his status? What's his status?

Hoot turns around in the Humvee, instantly assesses:

                    HOOT
          He's dead.

                    STRUECKER
          He's dead. He's dead.

McKnight and Steele both look stunned. Someone dead? That
just doesn't happen here.

INT. MATTHEW'S BLACK HAWK - SAME TIME

                    OBSERVATION BIRD PILOT
          The casualties aren't gonna make it.

INT. JOC - SAME TIME

Garrison glances down briefly, then back up, JOC silent.

INT. STRUECKER'S HUMVEE - CONTINUED

A stunned hush —— static -- from the speaker.

Then bullets hammer the outside of the truck --

                    STRUECKER
          Someone get on that .50!

Hoot is already climbing up into the turret.

                    HOOT
            It's mine.

OUTSIDE - Hoot sights a line of Somali gunmen up ahead and on
building tops. Hoot lets loose with a cruel sweep of the .50
caliber.

Huge slugs blast into the masonry -- dust and stone mixing
with crimson splatters of blood.

INT. WOLCOTT'S BLACK HAWK - SAME TIME

Wolcott flies above the city.

EXT. MOGADISHU STREET - SAME TIME

Mo'Alim drives a technical in reverse down a tight street,
keeping pace with Wolcott's circling Black Hawk.

Mo'Alim SLAMS the brakes and three Somalia jump out with RPG
tubes. Mo'Alim leaps off the vehicle. His men with the RPGs
await his signal. As the chopper turns in the sky --

INT. WOLCOTT'S BLACK HAWK - SAME TIME

Busch, Delta sniper, speaks into his headset --

                    BUSCH
          I got three guys with RPGs coming up on
          your side now!

EXT. MOGADISHU STREET - SAME TIME

Mo'Alim shouts, his hand drops, and his men FIRE. WHOOOSH!

INT. WOLCOTT'S BLACK HAWK - SAME TIME

Before Wolcott can react an RPG BOOMS into the tail rotor.
Busch's feet shoot out the cargo door.

                    WOLCOTT
          All right, we got a hit! Stay with it!

INT. JOC - SAME TIME

Garrison watches the drifting Black Hawk on a screen.

                    RADIOMAN (V.O.)
          Going down, he's hit, he's hit!

INT. WOLCOTT'S BLACK HAWK - CONTINUOUS

Wolcott and copilot Briley are the picture of calm as gauges
go blank and the helicopter begins to spin.

                    WOLCOTT
          Hey, Bull, you wanna pull those PCLs
          offline or what?

Briley, already struggling to pull the levers, returns
Wolcott's grin.

                    BRILEY
          Roger, they're off, Elvis.

                    WOLCOTT
          (remarkably calm)
          Six One going down…

FROM EVERYONE'S POSITIONS ON THE GROUND:

Eversmann, McKnight, Steele and others watch from their
vantage points as Super Six One drifts away from their fields
of view --

INT. WOLCOTT'S BLACK HAWK - CONTINUOUS

Bush grips a metal bar with one hand, chopper's spin
INTENSIFYING.

                    WOLCOTT
          Six One going down. Hold on!

EXT. CRASH SITE 1 - SAME TIME

IMPACT! The Black Hawk explodes into an enormous concrete
fountain, flips sideways, slams onto the road, nose burrowing
into the dirt, control panel crumpling, glass shattering
inward -- Wolcott and Briley killed instantly. Everything
enveloped in dust.

Somalis run away in every direction.

INT. JOC - DAY

Garrison looks at the screen. Frantic voices on the command
net echo in the room:

> VOICES (V.O.)
> We got a Black Hawk Down! We got a Black
> Hawk Down! We got a Black Hawk Down!

INT. MATTHEW'S BLACK HAWK - SAME TIME

> HARRELL
> Super Six one is down! We got a bird
> down in the city!

INT. DURANT'S BLACK HAWK - SAME TIME

Durant scans the horizon.

> VOICES (V.O.)
> We got a Black Hawk Down! We got a Black
> Hawk Down!

FLASH - to Atto in his cell, sitting perfectly still, cigar
smoke swirling around his head. It's as if he knows what's
happened...

INT. JOC - DAY

ON SCREEN - the crash.

> GARRISON
> (into headset)
> Get an MH—6 on-site, check for survivors.
> Send in the SAR bird. I want ground
> forces to move and secure a new perimeter
> around that crash site. Can you guide
> the convoy in there?

> HARRELL (V.O.)
> Ah, Roger that.

> GARRISON
> Well, move quick. The whole damn city
> will be coming down on top of them.

Harrell begins relaying the instructions down the chain to
the pilots.

EXT. CHALK ONE, HALWADIG ROAD - LATER

> STEEL
> Two Five, this is Six Four, over?

EXT. CHALK 4 CORNER - SAME TIME

Eversmann trying to find out what they're supposed to do now.

> EVERSMANN
> This is Two Five, over.

EXT. CHALK ONE, HALWADIG ROAD - CONT.

> STEELE
> Two Five, Chalk Four is closest to the
> crash site, over?

EXT. CHALK 4 CORNER - CONT.

> EVERSMANN
> Six Four. I can't see the crash site.
> Over.

EXT. CHALK ONE, HALWADIG ROAD - CONT.

Steele is trying to communicate with Eversmann on the radio.

> STEELE
> Two Five, it's too East of you. You
> won't find it. At least secure the area.
> Repeat, move your chalk on foot to crash.
> Check for survivors, secure the area.
> All other chalks will follow, over?
> (noting but static)
> Two Five, you read me, over?

EXT. CHALK 4 CORNER -

Eversmann can't take it any longer. Signals to his men.

> EVERSMANN
> Goucher, Strick. Get Twombly! Hey,
> there's a Black Hawk down. Twombly
> Nelson, you're gonna stay here, you're
> gonna hold this corner, then exit with
> the Humvees. Galentine, Schmid, you're
> coming with me. All right? Let's go!
> Move out!

> NELSON
> How come I gotta stay back here?

> EVERSMANN
> Because you're dependable. All right,
> let's go. Go!

CONTINUED:

Eversmann takes off with the rest of his Chalk: Galentine, Yurek, Goodale, Kurth, Smith, Doc Schmid, and Waddell.

                    NELSON
          I hate being dependable, man.

Steele looks down the block, sees a distant Eversmann and his Chalk leaving. He can't see Nelson and Twombly behind their cover. Steele thinks the message was received.

INT. JOC - LATER

                    GARRISON
          We just lost the initiative.

Garrison stares at the downed Black Hawk on the screen.

EXT. STREETS - DAY

Militia and irregulars emerge from alleys and buildings around the Bakara Market. As they begin moving east toward the crash we RISE UP above the buildings, see some of them parallel to the route Eversmann's small group is taking, just one block over --

                    EVERSMANN
          Let's go!

As they become exposed around a corner, they take on heavy fire. An RPG explodes at their feet. They return fire, throw grenades.

Little Birds provide cover from the sky, wipe out a Somali machine gunner, clearing the way for Eversmann's chalk.

                    EVERSMANN (CONT'D)
          Go!

They run and fire.

EXT. TARGET BUILDING - DAY

Somali snipers are still firing from rooftops across the street. Wex ducks gunfire. SANDERSON BLASTS the rooftops.

                    WEX
          We've still got guys inside.

                    SANDERSON
          All right, all right, I'm going to go to
          the crash.

                                        (CONTINUED)

CONTINUED:

                        WEX
            Okay. You take the rest of the team;
            I'll finish loading the prisoners.

Steele shouts to be heard.

                        STEELE
            Negative! We proceed to the crash site
            together! Secure the perimeter and wait
            for the Humvees! Roger, Sir!

                      MCKNIGHT
            Roger that.

                        STEELE
            I'll take the lead.

Sanderson stares down the block, impatient.

                  STEELE (CONT'D)
            Sir, are you receiving me?

                    SANDERSON
            I heard you. We should be leaving, sir.

As if to punctuate his point, an RPG nicks the hood of a
Humvee and explodes against the target building. Othic and
Joyce duck, McKnight doesn't. Debris rains down on the
Rangers of Chalk One and Delta men.

                    MCKNIGHT
            All right, we need to move out now! I'll
            finish loading the prisoners, pick you up
            at the crash site.

                      MEN
               (in unison)
            Roger!

                      STEELE
             Let's move out!

                    SANDERSON
             Come on, let's go!

Chalk One and Delta element begin moving on foot toward the
distant crash. McKnight loads up the prisoners.

EXT. STREET - DAY

Steele and his men are in the lead, Delta behind. In the
rear, hugging the walls, is Grimes. Sanderson yells back --

CONTINUED:

                    SANDERSON
          Hey, hey! Stay away from the walls,
          whoever you are!

But the walls seem safe to Grimes. He's not getting away
from them even if his life depended on it, which it does. He
chugs along behind the Delta to keep up as -- He hears a loud
FWOOOSH!, turns to see -- AN RPG, streaking right at him.
Grimes DUCKS behind a low wall as it ricochets and -- BA-
WHOOOM! -- hits right above his head.

Sanderson stops firing, looks back at Grimes who appears
behind him.

                    SANDERSON (CONT'D)
          You okay?

                    GRIMES
          Yeah!

EXT. TARGET BUILDING - DAY

McKnight and Maddox jump in the Humvee and take off with the
Somali prisoners.

                    MCKNIGHT
          Let's go, Maddox! Maddox, look at these
          little skinny bastards! You muther
          fuckers! Go, go, go, left, left, left,
          left!

Maddox steers with his shoulders hunched in fear.

EXT. CHALK 4 CORNER AND STREETS - LATE AFTERNOON

Nelson and Twombly, left behind at Chalk 4, are crouched
behind a burned-out technical, reloading. There are bodies
of Somali gunmen around it.

A Black Hawk flies overhead.

                    NELSON
          Twombly? Twombly!

                    TWOMBLY
          What?

                    NELSON
          I think they've forgotten us!

                    TWOMBLY
          What?

                                              (CONTINUED)

CONTINUED:

                    NELSON
          It doesn't matter.

INT. JOINT OPERATIONS CENTER - SAME

Garrison watches the grainy images from P3 Orion as Somali
militia run towards the downed Black Hawk.

               OBSERVATION BIRD PILOT (V.O.)
          Indigenous personnel move to the crash.

                    CRIBBS
          Say again, over?

               OBSERVATION BIRD PILOT (V.O.)
          A lot of people closing in.

                    GARRISON
          How far is Chalk Four from the crash
          site?

                    OPERATOR (O.S.)
          About six blocks, Sir.

                    GARRISON
          Well they need to haul ass!

INT/EXT WOLCOTT'S BLACK HAWK — DAY

Wolcott is dead. Dan Busch crawls out of the wreckage. He
fires, trying to keep Somali gunmen from the downed chopper.
Targets pop up. Everywhere. Busch hits every one, plugging
rounds into the fleeting forms of armed Militia.

INT. JOINT OPERATIONS CENTER - SAME

Garrison watches gunfire on the screen around the crash site.

EXT. CRASH SITE - CONT.

Busch takes a bullet in the knee and nearly goes down.

NEARBY - EVERSMANN'S GROUP

The chalk splits, moves to opposite sides of the street.
Gunfire erupts from the corner, Yurek, Kurth and Galentine
running for a burned—out car. Galentine drops his weapon as
he dives for cover.

                    EVERSMANN
          Scotty! Scotty, are you okay?

                                                    (CONTINUED)

CONTINUED:

Across the street, Eversmann watches, then glances ahead and sees the tip of a rifle poke out from behind the edge of a building.

Glancing back, he sees Galentine, obviously about to run back out to retrieve his weapon in the middle of the street.

> EVERSMANN (CONT'D)
> No! Don't go!

Galentine can't hear or can't understand and hurries out. To cover him, Eversmann has to step into the street, firing at the edge of the building.

They continue moving. Then a Technical comes up behind them, bullets flying.

Galentine looks at his hand, covered with blood. His thumb is hanging by a thread of skin.

EXT. STREETS — DAY

Eversmann and the others are firing nearly nonstop. It's chaos.

> YUREK
> Go, go, go!

Eversmann crosses the street, ducks behind Yurek. Fires in that direction. Yurek signals the others to move.

> YUREK (CONT'D)
> Go! Go!

The rest of the group continues along the block as Yurek cover fires at the approaching mob. He turns to follow them as

KRATAKRATAKRAK! AK-47 gunfire wails down at Yurek, he kicks in the tin door of the nearest structure he can find, diving into --

INT. SCHOOLROOM - SAME TIME

-- a cramped schoolroom, cluttered with terrified kids huddling in a corner with their 16 year-old teacher.

Bullets EXPLODE through the tin door.

Bullets ZING! through the tin, explode around the room.

Yurek puts his finger over his mouth to be quiet.

CONTINUED:

The teacher stares at him, nods. She gets the message.

Yurek sees a back door. Moves over to it. Turns to the kids, waves. One child waves back, smiles at him.

Peeks out. Clear. Steps outside.

EXT. BEHIND THE CLASSROOM - DAY

Pokes his head out to check the Street. Looks both ways as -- A SOMALI GUNMAN fires at him from one direction as -- The Somali's TEN YEAR OLD son, AK-47 too big for his little hands, FIRES from the other direction, poorly aimed bullets ricocheting off the crumbling alley wall, just missing Yurek, a bullet taking the heel of his boot off.

Yurek pulls his head back just in time as -- The SOMALI MAN groans, hit by ricochet of his son's bullets. The man crumples to the dirt, dying.

Yurek sees the kid run past him to his father, on his knees over his father, wailing, AK-47 forgotten. Yurek holds his gun on dying father and son. About to fire. Doesn't. Then runs.

EXT. HALWADIG ROAD - DAY

The McKnight Humvee convoy starts up Halwadig. A voice crackles through the radio:

                OBSERVATION BIRD PILOT (V.O.)
        Unit One, this is Six Four, you have to
        slow down.

INSIDE MCKNIGHT'S HUMVEE

                MCKNIGHT
        Romeo, Six Four, I need to know before I
        get to the god damned street!

INT. MATTHEWS C2 BIRD - SAME

              OBSERVATION BIRD PILOT
        You have to slow down, there's a delay
        from the time directions are relayed from
        P-3, to JOC, then to me.

INSIDE MCKNIGHT'S HUMVEE

McKnight yells back through the radio.

CONTINUED:

                    MCKNIGHT
          We can't slow down! We're taking heavy
          enemy fire! We can't slow down!

EXT. BASE HANGAR - DAY

Sizemore is among thirty technicians, mechanics and cooks,
all gathered around a big radio, listening with dawning
horror at the drama out there.

INT. JOINT OPERATIONS CENTER - LATER

                    GENERAL GARRISON
               (standing, to Cribbs)
          What in the hell is the status of
          Struecker's Humvees?

                    CRIBBS
          General Harrell, ETA to base, Strueker's
          column?

EXT./INT. STRUEKER'S COLUMN - DAY

The convoy rumbles down the road.   Thomas holds a bloody
Pilla. Hoot stands at the turret gun, no longer firing -- in
a daze.

EXT. CRASH SITE - DAY

Busch leans against the chopper wall surrounded by a dozen
dead Somali gunmen shot at close range. Busch's face is
gray. Blood streams down his nose.

INT. JOC - SAME

SILENCE. Garrison watches the Orion plane's grainy image of
Maier landing his Little Bird at the crash site.

EXT. CRASH SITE - DAY

A dust storm kicks up as Maier and his copilot Jones set the
Little Bird down in front of Wolcott's crashed Black Hawk.

EXT. ADJACENT ALLEY TO BLACK HAWK CRASH - LATER

Eversmann and his guys come around the corner. Through a
massive city archway, they can see Wolcott's downed chopper,
lying on its side. Little Bird whirling in front of it.

Eversmann motions for his men to follow him. They charge
through the enormous city gate, bullets slapping around them.

EXT. CRASH SITE - DAY

Clark and Jones run toward the crash from their Little Bird.
Finds Busch leaning against the Black Hawk, weapon aimed.

Jones and Clark throw Busch's arm over their shoulders, and
the three move to the chopper. Somali gunfire raining around
them.

EXT. ADJACENT ALLEY TO BLACK HAWK CRASH - SAME

                    EVERSMANN
          Galentine, you alright?
               (Galentine nods)
          Covering fire! Go!

                    GALENTINE
          We'll cover!

Eversmann and his team run in to the crash site. They are
now in an enormous open area, four roads leading out -- four
possible lanes of fire to worry about.

Jones and Clarke get the limp Dan Busch into the Little Bird
as Eversmann charges over, shouts:

                    EVERSMANN
          Hey, how many are in there?

                    JONES
          Two pilots are dead. Two crew chiefs are
          wounded. This guy's hurt bad. We gotta
          get out of here, now!

                    EVERSMANN
          Okay.

Jones helps Clarke inside, jumps in, Maier lifting off into
the swirling dust as RPGs explode around the Little Bird.

Eversmann crouches low, bullets pinging around him as he
dashes to the downed chopper. Sees Wolcott's dead body.

The Little Bird flies away.

A Technical ROARS down the street. A Ranger shoots a rocket
at it. It bursts into flames as Eversmann sprints from
Wolcott's Black Hawk, joins Smith and Goodale in a mortar
cavity carved into a wall.

                    EVERSMANN (CONT'D)
               (into radio)
          Two Six, Two Six, this is Two Five.
               (MORE)

                                        (CONTINUED)

CONTINUED:

      EVERSMANN (CONT'D)
  The guys are shooting up the technicals,
  over!

EXT. CORNER NEAR WOLCOTT CRASH SITE - CONT.

As Di Tomasso's Chalk 3 arrives at one of the cross streets,
he answers Eversmann.

      DI TOMASSO
  Two Six, Two Six, roger that!

      EVERSMANN
  Di Tomasso! Take the Southeast border,
  we'll set up a perimeter, over?

      DI TOMASSO
  Delta two Six, Roger that. Moving my men
  out. Move out!

Di Tomasso nods and waves his men to a structure on the
Southeast corner. They move and take immediate heavy fire.

      EVERSMANN
  Captain Steele, Captain Steele, come in!

Intercut to Steele -

      STEELE
  Go ahead Two Five, this is Six Four!

      EVERSMANN
  We got two wounded and we got both the
  pilots dead in the chopper. We need a
  medivac over here now!

      STEELE
  Two Five, they're telling me it's too hot
  to land the birds. You gotta secure the
  perimeter first, over.

      EVERSMANN
  Where are the Humvees?

      STEELE
  Advise Two Five the convoy will be there.
  They're encountering light resistance.
  Six Four out.

Eversmann signals to Kurth.

      EVERSMANN
  Kurth!

             (CONTINUED)

CONTINUED:

                    KURTH
          Let's go!

They move out.

EXT. BASE HANGAR - DAY

STRUECKER'S THREE HUMVEES PULL IN to the Hangar area.
Hundreds swarm toward them.

                    RANGER
          Hey, we need a medic! Hey, we need a
          medic immediately to get this last load
          in!

Bloody bodies are carried out of the Humvees on stretchers.

Sizemore, cast on his arm, watches as Pilla is taken out,
dead. Blackburn, broken. Half the others, bleeding.

IN A HUMVEE -- Hoot's head peers in. There's already the
buzzing of flies over the pools of blood and gristle.

INT/EXT. MCKNIGHT'S CONVOY - DAY

Light resistance? It's the fucking end of the world --
swarms of bullets raking the Humvee squad, RPGs streaking by
with deadly whispers, exploding into walls. A .50 gunner
slumps down in the turret, hit.

                    MCKNIGHT
          Get the .50 up! God dammit!

A Ranger tries, can't get through the bodies blocking the
way.

                    MCKNIGHT (CONT'D)
          All I see is a roadblock.

INT. MATTHEWS C2 BIRD - SAME TIME

                    HARRELL
          Alright, I'm going to have to figure out
          another way.

ON THE HUMVEE BEHIND - an RPG hits the back of the vehicle,
flinging Alberto Rodriguez, Wex and another man into the
street like unwanted toys during a child's tantrum.

                    MCKNIGHT
               (leaping out, shouts)
          Give me a defensive perimeter so we can
          load the wounded!

                                        (CONTINUED)

CONTINUED:

Joyce, Kowalewski and other Rangers leap out, firing at
windows, doorways, rooftops. Othic nearly steps on a hand in
the street, doesn't know whose it is. He'll figure it out
later; puts it in his pocket.

                    RANGER
          Fire your weapon, Othic!

McKnight comes upon the writhing Wex. The Delta Operator has
no lower half of his body.

Wex is muttering something, somehow still alive, reaching up
at McKnight, taking his hand and squeezing.

                    WEX
          Tell my girls they'll be okay.

McKnight watches him die. Then yells out.

                    MCKNIGHT
          Othic!

Othic runs low -- to McKnight's side.

                    MCKNIGHT (CONT'D)
          Medic!

Othic and a medic carry Wex, put him inside the Humvee..

Joyce returns fire. Then takes a shot in the back where he
removed the vest panel. Crumples to the street.

Kowalewski and McKnight drag Joyce's limp body toward the
trucks.

INT. MATTHEW'S BLACK HAWK - DAY

                    MCKNIGHT (V.O.)
          Get us off this fucking street!
               (into radio)
          Where's the crash site? Say again?

                    HARRELL
          Keep going straight 200 meters.

                    MCKNIGHT (V.O.)
          Okay.

INT. MCKNIGHT'S HUMVEE - CONT.

McKnight hops into the cab, bullets again exploding into the
convoy, SHOUTS to Maddox —

                                              (CONTINUED)

CONTINUED:

                    MCKNIGHT
          Let's go, let's go!

EXT. CHALK 4 CORNER AND STREETS - SAME

Silence. Nelson and Twombly, left behind at Chalk 4, are
crouched in their bunker, reloading. There are bodies of
Somali gunmen around it.

But now, there is nothing but sporadic gunfire on the corner.
Nelson glances back down the block toward the target house.

                    NELSON
          Hey, Twombles?

                    TWOMBLY
        What?

Twombly stands and moves over to Nelson.

                    NELSON
          Come here! The Humvees ain't coming
          back, dude.

                    TWOMBLY
          Really? Were we supposed to go to them?

                    NELSON
          I thought they were supposed to come to
          us.

                    TWOMBLY
          Shit, I think we were supposed to go to
          them.

                    NELSON
         Shit!

                    TWOMBLY
          Okay, let's go to the crash site.

                    NELSON
          Okay. Just don't fire that thing so
          close to my head. I can barely hear as
          it is.

                    TWOMBLY
         Okay, move out.

Nelson goes first. He makes it half a block before bullets
start ticking the walls around him. Twombly covers. Nelson
dives behind another smoldering automobile carcass, turns and
covers as Twombly dives in beside him.

                                      (CONTINUED)

CONTINUED:

Suddenly an armed figure appears across the street; Twombly
fires inches from Nelson's head. The gunman falls as the
enormous boom of the SAW rings in Nelson's ears. He yells --

                    NELSON
          WHAT DID I JUST TELL YOU? I SWEAR TO GOD
          IF YOU EVER...

Another figure appears, and Twombly has to fire again.

                    NELSON (CONT'D)
               (in pain)
          AH!

                    TWOMBLY
          You okay? You alright?

                    NELSON
               (can't hear a thing - shouting)
          What?

INT. BUILDING - DAY

Militia with RPGs strapped to their backs climb steps for a
better angle on the hovering Six Eight Black Hawk.

INT. SIX EIGHT BLACK HAWK - DAY

The Black Hawk takes fire.

                    SIX EIGHT PILOT
          Sunnavabitch. C2, this is Six Eight,
          we've been hit.

INT. MATTHEW'S BLACK HAWK - DAY

                    HARRELL
               (into radio)
          Super Six Eight, there is smoke coming
          from the top of your rotor. Advise you
          to come out now.

                    SIX EIGHT PILOT
          Roger.

EXT. 4TH FLOOR BUILDING - SAME

The Somalis set up to fire their RPGs at the Black Hawk.

INT. SIX EIGHT BLACK HAWK - SAME

> SIX EIGHT PILOT
> Art, I've got skinnies with RPG's at 12
> o'clock, can you see them?

Rangers slide down the ropes.

> RANGER 2
> Go, go!

> SIX EIGHT GUNNER
> Got 'em. Give me 90 degrees left.

EXT. 4TH FLOOR BUILDING - SAME

They're about to fire as the Black Hawk banks. Relentless
machine gun fire from the Black Hawk mows them down inside
the building.

INT. SIX EIGHT BLACK HAWK - SAME

> SIX EIGHT PILOT
> Six Eight, coming out.

He banks the chopper away.

> HARRELL (V.O.)
> Super Six Eight is out.

EXT. CHALK 4 CORNER AND STREETS - SAME

Eversmann runs for cover behind upended trucks.

> EVERSMANN
> Galentine! What's the situation in
> there?

INSIDE WOLCOTT'S DOWNED BLACK HAWK -

> GALENTINE
> Both pilots are dead.

> WILKINSON
> (into radio)
> Two Five, we can't move these guys now.
> We'll kill 'em just carrying 'em.
> (to other Medic)
> Stabilize in here?

> GALENTINE
> Roger!

(CONTINUED)

CONTINUED:

>   WILKINSON
>   Stabilize in here. Repeat, stabilize in
>   the bird, over.

BACK TO EVERSMANN

>   EVERSMANN
>   Understood Wilky, we got you covered,
>   over.

INT. MATTHEW'S BLACK HAWK - SAME

>   HARRELL
>   (into radio)
>   Super Six Four, come in and take
>   Wolcott's position.

INT. DURANT'S BLACK HAWK - SAME

>   DURANT
>   Roger. Six Four's inbound.

He banks back toward the city center. Passes over rooftops.

EXT. MOGADISHU STREET - SAME

Militants with RPGs fire at Durant's chopper.

An RPG missile streaks into Durant's chopper's tail. The
Black Hawk rocks violently from the hit. The gauges blink
but stay lit. Durant hears in his headset -

>   HARRELL (V.O.)
>   Super Six Four, you all right?

INT. DURANT'S BLACK HAWK - SAME TIME

>   DURANT
>   This is Super Six Four. We're good.

INT. MATTHEW'S BLACK HAWK - SAME TIME

>   HARRELL
>   You sure? You look like you got clipped
>   pretty good.

INT. DURANT'S BLACK HAWK - SAME TIME

Durant and his copilot, Frank, check the gauges again.

(CONTINUED)

CONTINUED:

                    DURANT
         Instrument panels are okay. No, we're
         good. Got a slight vibration in the
         pedals. But we're good.

INT. MATTHEW'S BLACK HAWK - SAME TIME

                    HARRELL
         All right. Put it down on the airfield,
         Super Six Four, have it checked out.
         Just to be safe.

INT./EXT DURANT'S BLACK HAWK - SAME TIME

                    DURANT
         Roger.

Durant banks away from the crash site, heads south toward
base, grid of narrow streets and alleys rushing beneath him.

OUTSIDE, the bent tail rotor is looser and rattling louder.

                    DURANT (CONT'D)
         Hey Ray, I'm getting a lot of movement in
         these pedals. Check the systems.

SUDDENLY -

THE ROTOR PIN PULLS FREE, slices through the gear box, and
the entire tail assembly evaporates in a blur.

Inside, there's a high whine as the airframe vibrates.
Durant tries to correct the spin with the pedals; Frank kills
the power with the ceiling levers.

                    DURANT (CONT'D)
         We lost the tail rudder! Six Four's
         going down. Six Four going down!

INT. JOC - SAME

SILENCE… Garrison watches the Orion plane's grainy image of
Durant's Black Hawk crashing. Eyes locked on the monitor -

MONITOR - Durant's chopper hits the ground, crumpling, twists
into the dirt like a whale on the beach, main rotor still
chopping at the air like a gasp.

After stunned silence in the JOC, Garrison finally speaks.

                                              (CONTINUED)

CONTINUED:

                    GARRISON
          Get Struecker's column back up there.
          They need to get to Durant's crash site,
          fast.

                    OPERATOR
          I'm on it.

                    GARRISON
          All of them.

                    HARRELL (V.O.)
          Super Six Four is down.

EXT. CRASH SITE — DAY

Militiamen and Rangers exchange gunfire. Eversmann glances
over at Galentine, ghostly white, listening to his radio.

                    EVERSMANN
          What?

Then Eversmann's hip radio squawks, and he hears the voices
on the command net:

                    RADIO VOICES
          Bird down! Super Six Four is down.

Eversmann, looks at the faces of his chalk.

                    EVERSMANN
          They talking about another hawk?

His men nod.

EXT. MOGADISHU CORNER/NEAR THE 4TH FLOOR BUILDING - DAY

Steele and his thirty some Rangers have entered a killing
zone. Spread all over the road, his men are pinned down by
gunfire from a fourth floor window in a building around the
corner. They can't move forward down the street.

DOWN THE STREET - Sanderson and his Delta (and Grimes) are
pinned down, waiting to move. Sanderson shouts through the
walkie talkie:

                    SANDERSON
          Captain Steele, we gotta move or we're
          gonna get pinned down!

INTERCUT to Steele -

CONTINUED:

                    STEELE
          We're moving as fast as we can! You let
          me do my job and you do yours! Over!

                    SANDERSON
          We're gonna get chewed up if we don't get
          off this street.

EXT. MOGADISHU CORNER/NEAR THE FLOOR BUILDING - DAY

Ruiz fires when he's suddenly lifted and thrown against a
wall, blood spraying out his back, bullet entering just under
his vest.

                    RUIZ
          Fuck! Fuck! Fuck, fuck, I fucking knew
          I was gonna get shot!

Steele and his Rangers are still pinned down. Steele hovers
over Ruiz.

                    STEELE
          Medic!

A Ranger MEDIC crouches along the street, gunfire blasting
over his head. Starts working on Ruiz.

DOWN THE BLOCK - as bullets whiz past he and his Delta team,
SANDERSON mutters to himself --

                    SANDERSON
          Fuck this.
               (into radio)
          Cap'n Steele, we'll take out the window,
          we'll rally point at the gray building.
          Coming through, Captain!

ON STEELE — he looks back at Sanderson and Delta down the
block behind him.

                    STEELE
          Sergeant!

                    SANDERSON
          All right, let's move, let's move!

SANDERSON clicks off the radio. Gives Delta command by hand
signals. The Delta team moves down the block.

Grimes looks behind him. No one there. He takes a deep
breath and hustles after Delta.

ON STEELE — his position is under BLISTERING fire.

                                        (CONTINUED)

CONTINUED: (2)

Sanderson and Delta - pass Steele and his beleaguered Rangers without a second glance. Grimes keeps following Delta.

KRATAKRATAKRAK! Bullets immediately track the Delta team from the fourth floor window.

                    SANDERSON (CONT'D)
          Move! Move! Move!

As DELTA move in a crouch alongside a five foot high earthen mound.

Bullets kick up plumes of dirt along the crest of the mound above Delta's heads as --

SANDERSON pulls a grenade, yanks the pin and runs up the earthen mound, hurls the grenade four stories into the open window -- a perfect toss.

A MOMENT LATER -- the room explodes, shredded Somali bodies hurtling outward. More bullets rain at them from every direction:

                    SANDERSON (CONT'D)
          Let's go! Let's move!

Grimes runs along the earthen mound again. More bullets rip past him as he runs.

Steele and his Rangers follow the Deltas.

                    STEELE
          Move it!

EXT. STABLE - DAY

Bullets rain down on Delta from every conceivable direction as they sprint to the first cover they can find. Sanderson is behind them and dives into --

INT. STABLE —

A STABLE - no living animals here. Carcasses, bones, piles of moldering hay, ratty couch in a corner. High stone courtyard walls protect them from Somali bullets.

Grimes, covered in concrete powder, runs inside.

                    SANDERSON
          Come on, come on! Let's go, let's go!
          Come on, bring 'em down!

INT/EXT STEELE'S STABLE COURTYARD - DAY

As Steele and other Rangers spill into the filthy stable
courtyard an RPG blasts the building. Rangers are helping
wounded comrades through the doorway, while groups of others
carry seriously wounded men.

                    SANDERSON
          Grab him! Move him! Move him out of
          here! Go, go, go!

Steele whirls on SANDERSON, furious.

                    STEELE
          What the fuck are you doing out there?

                    SANDERSON
          Doing my job! Look, we gotta get to that
          crash site! We gotta get on that street
          and we gotta move! Now you have got to
          keep up, Sir!

Steele says under his breath so the others won't hear:

                    STEELE
               (livid)
          We are combat ineffective. We've got too
          many dang wounded to move.

                    SANDERSON
          Then give me some of your shooters and
          that'll get us closer to the bird!

Steele nods. His eyes travel around the room. His Rangers
are blood spattered, dazed, shell-shocked. Most are frankly
terrified. His gaze falls on Grimes.

                    STEELE
          Grimes! You're with Chalk Four!

Grimes flinches.

                    GRIMES
          Yes, Sir!

Steele speaks to his Rangers, but he's looking right at
Sanderson as he says:

                    STEELE
          All right, who's going with Delta?
          Grimes joins with Sergeant Eversmann.

Grimes' face falls.

(CONTINUED)

CONTINUED:

>   STEELE (CONT'D)
>   The rest of you men secure the position.
>   Treat the wounded, and we'll wait for the
>   convoy. Then we'll rally at the crash
>   site. Roger!

The other Rangers breathe a sigh of relief. Sanderson gives
Grimes a once over. Shakes his head. This is who he gets?
Finally he sighs, grabs his weapon.

>   SANDERSON
>   My guys, let's go!

>   STEELE
>   All right, let's cover him!

A look from SANDERSON is all Delta needs to let them know
they're moving out. They start filing back out into the
dangerous streets.

Grimes heads to the door, uncertain. With a last look back
at Steele, Grimes readies himself. Then he runs after Delta.

EXT. STREET — DAY

Sanderson and Delta emerge from the stable, Grimes trailing.
Delta are fluid, moving from cover to cover, fanning out on
either side of the street. Grimes hustles after them.

EXT. CRASH SITE - LATE AFTERNOON

Silence. Strapped to the seat of his downed Black Hawk,
Durant slowly comes to.

INT./EXT. GOFFENA'S BLACK HAWK - DAY

Circling, Goffena and his copilot Yacone can see Durant's
downed Black Hawk below.

In back, also looking down at it, are Delta snipers Shughart
and Gordon.

There's a crowd moving toward the crash from several blocks
away.

GOFFENA RADIOS -

>   GOFFENA
>   Romeo; Six Two. I got two Delta snipers
>   volunteering to go in to secure Crash
>   Site 2, over.

(CONTINUED)

CONTINUED:

                    MATTHEWS (V.O.)
          No, Six Two, that is negative to the
          request.

INT. MATTHEW'S BLACK HAWK - SAME TIME

                    MATTHEWS
          We don't see anything moving down there
          now. We don't even know if anyone's
          alive. A ground team is being organized
          to go in now.

                    GOFFENA
          ETA of ground team, over?

                    MATTHEWS
          Ah, unknown. Not long. Do what you can
          from the air.

EXT. CRASH SITE - LATE AFTERNOON

Still trapped to his seat, Durant sees through the shattered
windshield the Black Hawk flying overhead.

ETX. BASE GARAGE - DAY

STRUECKER STANDS BEFORE THE BATTERED HUMVEES.

                    STRUECKER
          All right, gather around! All right,
          Durant's Six Four is down.
               (Rangers mutter in anger)
          We're going back in to get 'em.

Now there is a prolonged silence. Rangers look at him like
he's nuts. Three Humvees behind him are bloody Swiss cheese.

                    THOMAS
          That's crazy! Is there anyone alive on
          that?

Thomas looks at other Rangers, some just as scared as he is.

                    STRUECKER
          It doesn't matter. No one gets left
          behind. You know that.

                    HOOT
          We're wasting time here.

                    STRUECKER
          All right! Refit, max out ammo and
          grenades. You've got five.

                                        (CONTINUED)

CONTINUED:

SIZEMORE is gearing up, wearing unlaced boots, swimming in an enormous extra flak vest.

> STRUECKER (CONT'D)
> Sizemore, where the hell do you think you're going?

> SIZEMORE
> With you guys.

> STRUECKER
> Not with that cast on you're not.

Sizemore pulls out his survival knife and goes to cut off his cast.

> STRUECKER (CONT'D)
> All right, all right, all right. Go get your K-pak.

Struecker moves off to get ammo and sees Thomas' worried face.

> STRUECKER (CONT'D)
> Hey, talk to me.

> THOMAS
> I can't go back out there.

> STRUECKER
> Thomas, everyone feels the same way you do, all right? It's what you do right now that makes a difference. It's your call. Hooah!

Struecker walks off.

> THOMAS
> Hooah.

INT. BASE GARAGE - LATER

Hoot slaps in a magazine, already re—supplied with grenades and ammo. He grabs a bunch of night vision goggles, slips them in a pack. Rangers stare at him.

Struecker is grabbing ammo when Hoot pulls him aside.

> HOOT
> It'll probably help to wash the blood out of the Humvees.

EXT. BASE GARAGE — DAY

Struecker's Humvees are slowly pulling out, everyone, from
company cooks to mechanics running after it, geared up with
borrowed armor, leaping on, wanting to join in the fight.
Thomas watches Struecker's loaded Humvee.

                    BASE RANGER
               (running alongside)
          Sergeant Struecker, wait! Sergeant
          Struecker! Can I go, Sir?

                    STRUECKER
          You got some ammo?
               (the Ranger does)
          Hop in.

Struecker looks back at Thomas.

Thomas, taking a hit from his inhaler, finally summons the
courage, runs to catch up.

                    THOMAS
          Sergeant!

Pulls the door open and jumps in.

EXT. DARKENED STREET CORNER - SUNSET

Nelson and Twombly, still looking for crash site one, charge
to a corner. The random burst of gunfire keeps them on edge.

                    TWOMBLY
          Which way?

Twombly shrugs: which way? He motions down the street, left
or right?

Nelson looks down the street.

                    NELSON
               (shouting)
          That way I think.

                    TWOMBLY
               (whispering)
          Sshh! Don't talk so fucking loud!

Twombly hears something, coming down the block, a strange
sound. -- clop, clack, clop. Motions Nelson back. Sound
growing louder, closer.

                                             (CONTINUED)

CONTINUED:

Eyes wide, Twombly aims his SAW as ——A DONKEY comes clopping past, pulling a cart without a driver. The animal briskly trots past Twombly, who nearly blew it head off. Twombly motions to Nelson. They RUN.

DOWN THE BLOCK — on a different corner, YUREK is pressed against an alley wall, terrified, alone, eyes wide. Hears a ghostly, disturbing sound, coming closer -- clop, clop, clop.

Yurek prepares himself, gun aimed. The same donkey comes clattering into the alley, walks right up to the stunned Yurek.

> YUREK
> Nice donkey.

Yurek pats its head as he takes a look out into the wide intersection. Then he bolts -- RUNNING around a corner, down another block, around another corner.

TWOMBLY AND NELSON level their weapons at him and start shooting.

> YUREK (CONT'D)
> Rangers!

> NELSON
> Who?

> YUREK
> It's Yurek, you fucking assholes!

> TWOMBLY
> Fuck! No, we almost fucking killed you!
> Oh, come to us!

Yurek, completely out of breath; tries to speak.

> YUREK
> Fuck You! Come to me!

Twombly and Nelson run to Yurek.

> NELSON
> Sorry Sarge.

> TWOMBLY
> Okay, never mind. You brought the NOD,
> right?

Yurek gives him a weary Look. Gasps out --

CONTINUED: (2)

                    YUREK
          No. No, I didn't bring it. And you want
          to know why? 'Cause you said: You're not
          gonna need that, dude, we'll be back in a
          half hour.

                    TWOMBLY
          Man, I wasn't saying it to you.

                    YUREK
               (looks at Nelson)
          Nelson, cover this way.

Nelson doesn't hear him.

                    TWOMBLY
          Man, we're gonna need night vision.

Yurek grabs Nelson. Nelson turns around.

                    YUREK
          What's the matter with you?

                    NELSON
          Huh?

                    TWOMBLY
          Oh, he's deaf. It's my fault, I... We
          really need to get out of here.

                    YUREK
          We can't be far from the crash. Which
          way?

                    TWOMBLY
          I thought you might know.

They take off down the street.

EXT. CRASH SITE - DAY

Eversmann's men are shooting constantly, trying to keep the
growing crowd of Somalis from the downed chopper.

                    EVERSMANN
               (To Galentine)
          Give me Nelson and Twombly now!

Galentine nods and clicks the handset of his radio, shouting
over the sounds of gunfire.

                                                  (CONTINUED)

CONTINUED:

                    GALENTINE
          Nelson...Twombly, come in! This is
          Galentine. Over. Nelson, Twombly, come
          in, this is Galentine! We need the
          position of the convoy, over?

Galentine shouts in frustration:

                    GALENTINE (CONT'D)
          I can't raise them, Sergeant! I can't
          raise them!

Eversmann swears under his breath as bullets EXPLODE over his
head.

                    EVERSMANN
          We gotta get the fuck out of here and
          evac!

                    GOODALE
          No, we can't move 'em. We're staying
          right here until the convoy gets here!
          Understood?
              (to all his men)
          We stay with the plan. Understood?

                    EVERSMANN
          Let's get back to the stronghold! Come
          on!

INT. JOINT OPERATIONS CENTER - LATER

Cribbs points to the map of Mogadishu. A big X represents
Wolcott's crash, another, further away, Durant's crash.

                    CRIBBS
          Ground forces have occupied several
          buildings along Marehan Road — they're
          all spread out. Eversmann's Chalk Four
          has set up a perimeter around Wolcott's
          crash site, here.
              (marks a spot)
          Di Tomasso is in the adjacent structure.
              (marks a more distant spot))
          Captain Steele and about forty men of
          Rangers are here, a couple blocks away.
          They're banged up pretty bad. He's set
          up a casualty collection point. I, I
          don't think they're gonna be able to
          move. Sergeant Sanderson and a small
          Delta team are moving from Steele's
          position to the crash site as we speak.

EXT. STREET NEAR CRASH - SUNSET

Sanderson is behind wreckage made by a mortar blast. He sees
Grimes near him, wonders briefly where he came from.

                    SANDERSON
          When this guy stops firing, I'll have
          four seconds to get to their corner.
          Cover me. Go!

Grimes nods as bullets SLAM into the wall above them. Grimes
runs forward.

The gunfire pauses.

Before Sanderson can move, Grimes has leapt out of the
crater.

                    GRIMES
          I got it!

GRIMES - charging the corner, seemingly taking forever to get
there. He rounds the corner and comes face to face with --
TWO SOMALI gunman, frantically trying to change magazines as
they see Grimes sliding to a stop before them. They slap in
the mags, raise their weapons, but -- Grimes waves a burst of
gunfire over them.

Grimes turns to SANDERSON -

                    SANDERSON
                 (shouting)
          RPG!

An RPG slams into the wall behind Grimes, burying him in
debris. This time he must be dead.

Sanderson charges to the mound of rubble, tossing aside
thirty-pound chunks of mortar and concrete. Sanderson pulls
Grimes out, dazed, hair blackened, helmet gone.

                    SANDERSON (CONT'D)
          You all right? You okay, man?

                    GRIMES
          Yeah! I can hear bells ringing.

Sanderson gives Grimes a nod and a thumbs up.

                    SANDERSON
                 (laughs)
          Come on, come on! Let's go!

                                              (CONTINUED)

CONTINUED:

Sanderson helps Grimes up.

INT./EXT. GOFFENA'S BLACK HAWK - LATE AFTERNOON

A crowd scatters from the low-flying Black Hawk but then
reforms again, heading toward Durant's crashed chopper.
Goffena sweeps around to make another pass.

> GOFFENA
> Romeo, Shughart and Gordon again request
> permission to secure until convoy
> arrives, over.

INT. JOC -SAME TIME

Garrison watches crowds of Somalis charge down the street on
the screen.

INT. MATTHEWS C2 BIRD - SAME TIME

Matthews can barely hear Goffena over the frantic voices of
the command net. He reaches out and SHUTS down all radio
channels. Silence except for rotors. Speaks to Harrell:

> HARRELL
> General, crowd's in the hundreds now.
> From where they are, they can see it
> clearer than any of us. They know what
> they're asking.

INT. JOC — SAME TIME

Silence except for the static. Finally ——

> GARRISON
> Let me talk to them.

INT. GOFFENA'S BLACK HAWK - SAME TIME

Shughart and Gordon hear over their headsets --

> GARRISON (V.O.)
> This is Garrison. I want to make sure
> that ya'll understand what you're asking
> for so say it out loud.

> GORDON
> We're asking to go in to set up a
> perimeter until ground support arrives.

INTERCUT to Garrison -

CONTINUED:

>   GARRISON
>   Now you understand I can not tell you
>   when that might be. It could take quite
>   a while.

>   SHUGHART
>   Roger that.

>   GARRISON (V.O.)
>   And you still want to go in?

>   GORDON
>   Yes, sir.

                                        BACK IN THE JOC -

Garrison chews on this for a moment. Then:

>   GARRISON
>   Colonel Harrell.

>   HARRELL (V.O.)
>   Yes, General.

>   GARRISON
>   It's your call.

>   HARRELL (V.O.)
>   Roger that. Goffena? Put 'em in.

                              BACK IN GOFFENA'S BLACK HAWK -

Goffena turns and gives Shughart and Gordon the thumbs up.

INT. DURANT'S BLACK HAWK - LATER

Visible through the windscreen, Durant looks up at the Delta
snipers in the chopper above and sees Goffena's Black Hawk
fly off.

EXT. MOGADISHU STREETS - LATER

McKnight's convoy rolls through a hail of gun fire.

INT. MCKNIGHT'S HUMVEE - CONT.

McKnight shakes his head as casings rain down on him from the
gun turret above.

>   MCKNIGHT
>   Mother fucker, mother fucker!

The Humvee takes fire from all sides.

INT. FIVE TON TRUCK - CONT.

A shaft of light tears through the door and into Othic's
shoulder. A round hits Othic in the knee. He screams and
then sees an RPG coming straight at the driver's door.

                    OTHIC
          RPG!

The RPG comes crashing through the metal — but doesn't
explode.

The convoy stops.

McKnight walks to Alphabet's truck and yanks the door open.

Dazed, Othic looks to Kowalewski: there's a foot long RPG
missile embedded in his chest, fins sticking out his left
side, arm severed off. Kowalewski is dead.

                    OTHIC (CONT'D)
          There's a fucking bomb in him, Sir.

                    MCKNIGHT
          Othic, calm down, god dammit! That's
          live ammo! Now get out!

Othic jumps out of the Humvee. McKnight gets Kowalewski out
of the truck.

                    MCKNIGHT (CONT'D)
          Come on, let's move him. Son of a bitch!

The men lift the dead Kowalewski to a Humvee.

                    MCKNIGHT (CONT'D)
          All right, lift him up, lift him up.
          Easy, easy, all right, get him in there.
          Good, good, easy, easy!

Othic tries to climb into the Humvee as well as the men
gingerly load Kowalewski in to the back.

                    MCKNIGHT (CONT'D)
          Get back in that truck and drive.

                    OTHIC
          I'm shot, Colonel.

                    MCKNIGHT
          Everybody's shot. We need the prisoners.
          Let's go!

INT. MATTHEWS C2 BIRD - LATER

A voice crackles through the radio.

>   RADIO VOICE (V.O.)
>   C3 says to take Halwadig and take it
>   straight.

>   HARRELL
>   McKnight, we need you to turn around and
>   head back to Halwadig.

INTERCUT to McKnight - radios back --

>   MCKNIGHT
>   You're shitting me. We just came through
>   there. There's gotta be a better way!

>   HARRELL
>   That's the info I'm getting from JOC.
>   You need to turn around and head back.

McKnight looks at Maddox. Shakes his head.

>   MCKNIGHT
>   Roger that, roger that. I cannot believe
>   this shit.
>   (sighs)
>   Turn us around, Maddox.

>   MADDOX
>   They're trying to get us fucking killed,
>   aren't they, Sir?

>   MCKNIGHT
>   Just get it over with. Drive!

>   MADDOX
>   God damn!

>   MCKNIGHT
>   Just, just get us outta here, god dammit!
>   Drive!

Resigned, Maddox executes a K-turn. The column slowly turns
around.

Maddox hits the gas. They head right back into the fray.

Hell begins anew. HUNDREDS of rounds RAKE the vehicles,
punching holes through metal.

The windshield SHATTERS, spraying glass into Maddox's face.

                                        (CONTINUED)

CONTINUED:

             MADDOX
     AHHH! I'm blind.
        (grabs the wheel)
     Keep your foot on the gas!

A bullet PINGS into the doorframe next to McKnight, slices into his neck. Blood sprays the dashboard.

             MCKNIGHT
     Fuck!

He presses a hand on his wound.

Maddox's face is a mass of blood, hands to his eyes. But he keeps stepping on the pedal, McKnight steering, neck bleeding.

EXT. CRASH SITE - LATE AFTERNOON

Still strapped to his seat Durant sees the Black Hawk flying overhead.

Hears Somali voices, yelling, coming closer. Tries to reach back for his rifle, grunts in agony, back damaged. Can't get to it. Sweating, reaching, swearing in pain as -- SOMALI FACES appear in his windscreen, raise their AKs at him. Durant raises one arm to protect himself as he fires -- the first Somali gunmen's chest EXPLODES.

Gordon and Shughart land. GUNFIRE raging as they charge toward the chopper.

DURANT - Somalis charge the Black Hawk. Durant fires away.

He sees Shughart and Gordon rounding the corner, boots slapping earth. Appearing like angels. They fire at the approaching Somalis. Shughart bangs on the Black Hawk.

             SHUGHART
     Friendlies!

Shughart checks Frank's pulse.

             DURANT
     God, it's good to see!

             GORDON
     Oh, it's good to see you. How bad?

             DURANT
     My leg's broken. My back feels kinda
     weird.

                                      (CONTINUED)

CONTINUED: (2)

                         GORDON
            We gotta get you outta here, buddy. I'm
            pulling him out. Cover!

Gordon gently lifts Durant from the chopper and he screams in
pain. Shughart covers.

                         SHUGHART
            I'm gonna put you down.

They prop him against a wall.

                         GORDON
            Cross, we're at the Six Four crash sight,
            securing the perimeter. You all right?

                         DURANT
            Yeah, I'm good.

Shughart puts Durant's MP-5 in his hands.

                         GORDON
            You're locked and loaded. If you see
            anyone come around these corners -- you
            watch your back.

Shughart and Gordon run back to the crash site.

                         DURANT
            Hey! Where's the rescue squad?

Gordon whirls, says:

                         SHUGHART
            We're it!

Durant is left alone, cradling his MP-5.

INT. STABLE - DAY

Steele talks to Harrell on the radio.

                         STEELE
            C2, you keep talking about a convoy, I
            would dearly like to know where in sam
            hill that is, over?

                         HARRELL (V.O.)
            Perimeter has to be tighter for the
            convoy. You're too far from the crash.
            They spread out like that, and you're all
            liable to be overrun. Over.

                                        (CONTINUED)

CONTINUED:

> STEELE
> C2, if I use two men for each wounded, I
> still got nobody left to shoot. Now,
> we're staying where we are, over?

Ruiz sighs.

EXT. STREETS - DAY

In the lead Humvee of the Lost Convoy, Maddox mops at his
bloodied face while McKnight, peering out the broken
windshield, drives, his neck a mess of blood…

McKnight finds himself in front of a familiar building — the
target building.

> MCKNIGHT
> Stop, stop, stop, stop, stop, Maddox,
> stop!

INT. MCKNIGHT'S HUMVEE - CONT.

Maddox face is a bloody mess. He slams on the brakes.

> MCKNIGHT
> (resigned, into radio)
> Son of a bitch! Romeo Six Four, we're
> right back where we started! I'm running
> low on ammo. I got many wounded,
> including me. Vehicles that are barely
> running.

> HARRELL (V.O.)
> Okay, Danny, I need a no b.s. assessment
> here. Can you get to the crash site?

McKnight hears groans of the wounded in back, sounds of tire
rims grinding on the road, bullets smacking into metal.

> MADDOX
> Colonel, I can't see shit.

> MCKNIGHT
> Negative. With the amount of wounded we
> have, we'd do more harm than good. We
> need to come back to base, rearm and
> regroup and then we can go back out.

> HARRELL
> Roger.

INT. JOC - SAME TIME

Monitoring this, Garrison speaks into a headset.

                    GARRISON
          C2...bring 'em back. Get 'em out of
          there!

                    HARRELL
          Roger, return to base.

INT. MCKNIGHT'S HUMVEE - CONT.

McKnight shouts to the wounded men in back.

                    MCKNIGHT
          We're going home. Let's go! Left! Go,
          go, go, go, god dammit! Run that mother
          fucker over! Go, go, go! Left, left,
          left, left, left! We're gonna be home in
          a second, we're gonna be home in a
          second. Hang on! God dammit, you guys
          hang on!

INT. EVERSMANN'S POSITION - LATER

Galentine throws his radio headset down.

                    EVERSMANN
          What's up?

                    GALENTINE
          They're sending 'em back. The convoy's
          headed back to base camp.

Some of the other men hear it and look over to Eversmann.
What now? What does he suggest now?

                    WADDELL
          Oh, now that makes sense, don't it? We
          need to exfil the wounded now, and get
          the hell outta here before its too late!

                    SMITH
          If Colonel McKnight went back to base,
          then he had a damn good reason. It
          changes nothing.

Right now, some of his men don't seem too convinced.

(CONTINUED)

CONTINUED:

>   EVERSMANN
>   All right, listen up. We're gonna hold
>   the perimeter. We're gonna hold the
>   strongpoint. Hooah!

Eversmann looks at each man, into the wide, scared eyes of
Smith, Galentine, Kurth, Goodale, Waddell and Doc Schmid.

>   MEN
>   (in unison)
>   Hooah!

>   EVERSMANN
>   Conserve your ammo. Only shoot at what
>   you can hit. Hooah?

>   MEN
>   (in unison)
>   Hooah!

His men stare out into the city, gripping weapons. Fear
turning to anger, confusion into focus.

>   EVERSMANN
>   The convoy's gonna come. We're gonna get
>   home.

EXT. DURANT'S CRASH SITE - DUSK

Delta snipers GORDON AND SHUGHART are sprawled out under the
ruined chopper tail, ammo magazines piled beside them.

THEY FIRE at endless targets. Countless AK—47 muzzle flashes
flare from every direction. A living nightmare.

>   GORDON
>   Loading.

Gordon slaps in an ammo mag, Shughart covering them.

GORDON'S POV — firing again, he hits EVERYTHING. Militia are
nailed in the head, chest, some targets 100 yards away.

>   GORDON (CONT'D)
>   Randy, I need a pistol mag!

Shughart throws Gordon the mag and he loads it.

>   SHUGHART
>   Loading.

GORDON FIRES AT MILITIA.

OVERHEAD - THOUSANDS OF SOMALIS edge closer to them -- an armed, furious mob that will stop at nothing.

Shughart grabs a magazine.

                    SHUGHART
          Loading.

Gordon grabs a magazine. Pile of ammo getting smaller.

ON THE PILE OF MAGAZINES - Gordon reaches for the last one.

                    GORDON
          Randy, last mag!

Crowd of Somalis now charging at them, making suicide runs. Too many of them.

Gordon takes a bullet in the head.

                    SHUGHART
          Gordy!

Shughart runs in to Gordon.

                    SHUGHART (CONT'D)
          Fuck!

EXT. DURANT'S CRASH SITE - DUSK

Durant is firing his MP-5 at dozens of Somalis. Every time he fires they disappear behind walls. Shughart scrambles back to Durant, gives him a CAR-15 rifle. The weapon is covered in blood. Gordon's.

Shughart touches Durant's shoulder.

                    SHUGHART
          Good luck.

Shughart again crawls under the chopper as -- SOMALIS peer around the corner. Durant fires at them. Two more gunmen poke their heads around. Durant fires again.

EXT. MOGADISHU STREETS - MOMENTS LATER

Hundreds of Somalis race towards the crash site.

INT. JOC - LATER

Garrison speaks to Cribbs in the subdued JOC.

(CONTINUED)

CONTINUED:

                        GARRISON
          We need the 10th Mountain in there.
          Everything they got. Pakistanis, Malays,
          I want their tanks and APCs.

On the monitors, Garrison can see roadblocks going up in the
streets surrounding Wolcott's crash, boxing the Americans in.

                        CRIBBS
          They still don't know we've gone in.

                        GARRISON
          Look. We have stirred up the hornet's
          nest here. We're fighting the entire
          city. I want every vehicle possible. If
          it has four wheels and armor, get it!
          Get everything.

Garrison and Cribbs consult a map of Mogadishu, hostile and
safe areas outlined in red and green.

                        GARRISON (CONT'D)
          Now once they've assembled, we need to
          move our men out of the hostile area and
          back to The Pakistani stadium, the safe
          zone. Now let's go!

                        CRIBBS
          (Cribbs nods -- sounds good)
          Roger that, boss.

Cribbs leaves the room.

INT. DURANT'S BLACK HAWK - CONT.

SOUNDS OF a FRANTIC FUSILLADE echoes from the other side of
the chopper. Shughart's gun roaring. AK-47s firing back.

The SOMALIS charge toward Shughart. Fires a quick burst.
The Somalis fall dead as -- Shughart takes several bullets at
close range.

SOUNDS of the fusillade on the other side of the chopper
continue. Then...the shooting stops.

A strange lull....nothing... then hundreds of Somalis swarm
from either side of the helicopter.

EXT. DURANT'S CRASH SITE - CONT.

A SOMALI pops his head around the corner. Durant fires,
dropping him. Click! The weapon goes dry as Durant runs out
of ammo.

                                              (CONTINUED)

CONTINUED:

The crowd drags the wounded crew from the chopper, tearing off clothes, boots.

Durant has time to do one last thing: pulls a snapshot of his wife and infant child from his flight suit pocket.

Somalis finally see him in the corner. They descend upon him.

A rifle butt slams into Durant's face, breaking his nose and the orbital bone of his left eye. He's kicked, spit on, uniform ripped at, crowd trying to pull him apart.

The photo of his family falls from his grasp. In a haze of pain, he crawls after the snapshot. A boot stomps on his hand, photo kicked away.

KRATAKRATAT! Gunfire erupts over the crowd's head. Everything stops as MO'ALIM hops down from a technical skidding to a halt, .50 caliber smoking.

A big Somali with him, FIRIMBI, shouts into a megaphone;

                    FIRIMBI
            (in Somali, subtitled)
        Back up! Mohamed Farrah Aidid claims
        this prisoner alive.

Durant opens his eyes, sees Mo'Alim's elaborate tattoos, his teeth stained orange and black from khat. As Firimbi again shouts into the megaphone, Mo'Alim fires his AK-47 over the crowd's head. Somalis retreat as Durant passes out again.

EXT. BASE — DUSK

McKnight's convoy arrives, battered and bloody.

McKnight watches his men, many of them injured themselves, unload the wounded and dead.

Wex is dead. Joyce. Several others.

EXT. STREETS - DUSK

Struecker's convoy keeps moving but is making little progress; roadblocks everywhere, constant volleys of gunfire.

                    HARRELL (V.O.)
        See where those tires are burning? All
        that black smoke?

                                              (CONTINUED)

CONTINUED: (2)

                    STRUECKER
          Roger, I can see it, but I can't get
          there. Over.

They can see the smoke in the sky, but all the streets
leading there are strategically blocked.

INT. MATTHEWS C2 BIRD - SAME TIME

                    HARRELL
          Go a hundred meters past it, that's the
          crash.

INTERCUT to Struecker -

                    STRUECKER
          Negative. You don't understand, it's
          roadblock after roadblock. You have to
          find us another route. Over.

                    HARRELL (V.O.)
          There ain't one. The only other route is
          all the way around the city.

                    STRUECKER
          Roger that, we'll take it.

                    HOOT
               (grabs the radio handset)
          Kilo Six Four, this is Kilo One One,
          request permission to move to crash Site
          number 2 on foot. Over.

As Hoot reloads and waits for an okay, Struecker regards him
like he's nuts. To Struecker --

                    HARRELL (V.O.)
          Green light, Kilo One. Green light.

                    HOOT
          Stop the vehicle. Let me out.

Struecker slows. Hoot jumps out. Raps on the side of the
Humvee for a couple of other Delta to join him, including.
Sizemore. The four run down a side street.

EXT. MOSQUE TOWER - SUNSET

The voice comes from a loudspeaker mounted on the mosque. An
unseen holy man intoning the evening prayer -

INT. EVERSMANN'S GROUP - SUNSET

Eversmann hears the lone voice, too. Then other voices join
in from mosque loudspeakers elsewhere in the city.

EXT. STEELE'S POSITION- SUNSET

Steele and his men listen to it in their stable.

Wilkinson adjusts the drip on an IV bag. Fluids slowly drip
into the crew chief's veins. Tries to relax the other dazed
crew chief as he works:

> WILKINSON
> After I'm finished with this, I'll whip
> you boys up some margaritas. The usual,
> blended, no salt?

INT. EVERSMANN'S GROUP - SUNSET

Eversmann's group listens to the evening prayer.

> RADIO VOICE (V.O.)
> Somebody's always gotta ruin a party,
> huh?

> KURTH
> (in Somali)
> Meta pa pa.

Smith throws Kurth his canteen.

EXT. OTHER STREET - SUNSET

As the voices echo, Sanderson and his group keep moving
through narrow slum streets. He radios Eversmann --

> SANDERSON
> Eversmann, come in. Eversmann.

INTERCUT - with Eversmann, his chalk in strategic positions
outside his Alamo building.

> EVERSMANN
> Roger. Who is this?

> SANDERSON
> Sanderson. Do not, I say again, do not
> fire to the east. We are coming to you.

> EVERSMANN
> (into radio)
> Understood.
> (MORE)

(CONTINUED)

CONTINUED:

                    EVERSMANN (CONT'D)
          Di Tomasso and his men are on the
          southeast corner. We need you on the
          northeast building.

                    SANDERSON
          Roger, we'll take it.

                    EVERSMANN
          Hey, watch out for skinnies. They're all
          over the rooftops.

Sanderson motions for his men to move forward.

Eversmann turns to his men --

                    EVERSMANN (CONT'D)
               (quietly)
          Hold your fire to the east!

Sanderson's men move towards the northeast building. Grimes
bringing up the rear.

                    SANDERSON
          Follow him! Go, go.

EXT. DOWN THE BLOCK - SUNSET

Twombly, Nelson and Yurek are sixty yards and across the
street from Eversmann's position. They dash out, the hulking
shape of Wolcott's Black Hawk visible in the intersection.

                    YUREK
          Eversmann. It's Yurek, I got, I got
          Nelson and Twombly with me. We got the
          chopper in sight. Where are you?

INTERCUT - with Eversmann.

                    EVERSMANN
          We're on the Southwest corner. Where the
          hell have you been? Are you okay?

Nelson takes ammo from a dead Somali lying at their feet.

                    YUREK
          Yeah. Hold your fire. We're coming in.

                    YUREK (CONT'D)
          We gotta go.

                    TWOMBLY
               (shouting)
          Shawn, Shawn, listen. Sergeant Yurek's
          gonna run first.
                    (MORE)

                                        (CONTINUED)

CONTINUED:

                    TWOMBLY (CONT'D)
              (Yurek's look says, I am?)
          Now when he gets across the street, he's
          gonna turn around and he's gonna cover
          you as you run. Listen closely - when
          you get there, you're gonna turn around
          and you're gonna cover me. Okay?

Nelson nods, but Twombly isn't really sure he understands.

                    TWOMBLY (CONT'D)
          Now you're not just gonna run to
          Eversmann's position, you're going to
          stop. You're gonna turn around and you
          are gonna cover me. It's important you
          understand that.

Nelson nods again, but it's even less convincing this time.
Twombly glances to Yurek.

                    TWOMBLY (CONT'D)
          Okay, you ready?

                    YUREK
          Yeah, I guess.

Yurek RUNS right through the center of the street.

BACK ON NELSON - getting ready --

                    TWOMBLY
          Hey, hey! Don't forget.

                    NELSON
              (shouting)
          What?

                    TWOMBLY
          Don't forget.

Nelson can't hear him. Twombly shrugs, Oh, fuck it, go.
Nelson runs. He makes it across the street, turns, sets and
covers Twombly's run perfectly.

ON EVERSMANN - he, Smith, Kurth, Goodale, Galentine and
Waddell watch as Yurek hauls ass.

                    GALENTINE
          I got them in my sights, Sarge. They're
          coming up on the west gate. I see 'em.

                    EVERSMANN
          Let's move out.

CONTINUED: (2)

                              YUREK
                   You gonna cover us Sergeant?

Eversmann radios back.

                              EVERSMANN
                   We got ya.

Yurek makes it across to them, turns, sets to cover Nelson.

                              TWOMBLY
                   Nelson.

PROVIDING COVER — as Nelson runs across.

Eversmann sees Somali's aiming but it's too late to warn
Twombly, who charges across the courtyard.

                              EVERSMANN
                   Fuck!

WHUMP! a Somali bullet hits Twombly in the back, right on
the bandolier of SAW bullets wrapped around him. Three SAW
rounds explode, lighting Twombly up like a human firecracker.

SMITH charges into the swarm of Somali gunfire, out into the
street to get Twombly --

                              SMITH
                   Twombly!

                              EVERSMANN
                   Smith, no!

Smith yanks Twombly to his feet and pulls him along, almost
to Eversmann before -- bullets trace a path up the street, a
round SMACKING into Smith's thigh, blood spraying the street.
Smith goes down.

                              SMITH
                   Oh, God, I'm hit!

Eversmann runs past the stumbling Twombly, ducks gunfire as
he grabs Smith, drags him the rest of the way and --

INT. - ALAMO HOUSE - CONT.

Inside, where they carry him to a table.

                              EVERSMANN
                   One, two, three. You're all right,
                   you're all right. You're all right. All
                   right?

                                              (CONTINUED)

CONTINUED: (3)

Doc Schmid immediately gets to work. Smith moans in pain.

                    SCHMID
I need pressure on this wound. Pressure,
okay? We're gonna need more Curlex
gauze. I need more men in here.

                    EVERSMANN
Twombly! Nelson.

                    SMITH
Oh man, that really, that really hurts!

                    SCHMID
I need that chair, that chair! Pressure,
get that pressure on it. Okay, let me
have a look, let me have a look. All
right, all right. Let me get a look at
that.

Rips Smith's pant leg, is spurted with arterial spray.
Blinks through it to get his kit open. Stuffs Curlex gauze
into Smith's gaping wound.

                    SMITH
Oh, oh, what the fuck is that?

Eversmann presses it into the wound but it's like trying to
cover a fire hose with a mattress. Schmid shoves more Curlex
at Eversmann as he readies an IV.

                    SCHMID
Hold that down. I need a medivac now.

                    EVERSMANN
Galentine! Galentine, get me Captain
Steele!

INT. STABLE - STEELE'S POSITION - LATER

Steele kneels down to check on Ruiz.

                    STEELE
Sergeant, sergeant Ruiz, how're you
doing?

Ruiz is spitting up blood.

                    RUIZ
They're not gonna come and get us.
They're not gonna come for us.

(CONTINUED)

CONTINUED:

                    STEELE
       I need you to suck it up Sergeant. I
       need you to focus for me. All right, can
       you do that? Now, can you hold your
       weapon?

                    RUIZ
       Yes sir.

                    STEELE
       If anybody comes through that door, you
       give 'em two in the chest and one in the
       head.

Steele hands Ruiz his weapon.

                    STEELE (CONT'D)
       You understand?

                    RUIZ
       I'm still willing to fight, Sir.

Steele's radio crackles:

                    EVERSMANN (V.O.)
       Captain Steele, Captain Steele,

INTERCUT - with Eversmann.

                    EVERSMANN (CONT'D)
       I need a medivac in here now. Corporal
       Smith's been hit.

                    STEELE
       Hold on Two Five.

                    RUIZ
       Still willing to fight.

                    EVERSMANN
       Captain Steele, he's hurt pretty bad.

                    STEELE (V.O.)
       Ah, Two Five, we got wounded too. You're
       just gonna have to maintain your
       situation, over?

Smith yells in agony.

                    SCHMID
       If he doesn't get to a hospital in a
       half—hour, he's in trouble.

                             (CONTINUED)

CONTINUED: (2)

                        STEELE (V.O.)
          C-2, this is Six Four. I'm requesting an
          immediate medical medivac for a
          critically wounded at Chalk Four's
          location, over.

INT. JOC - SAME TIME

                        HARRELL (V.O.)
          Command Chalk Four is requesting medivac.

                        GARRISON
          We can't risk it. It's still too hot.

                        HARRELL (V.O.)
          Captain, we can not send in medivac at
          this time. Sit tight, over.

INT STABLE - STEELE'S POSITION DAY - SAME TIME

Steele's resigned voice:

                        STEELE
          Two Five, this is Six Four. It's a
          negative on the medivac. It's not
          possible. JOC can not risk another bird.
          You're just gonna have to hold on. Six
          One out.

Long silence. Eversmann puts the radio back as Smith writhes
in pain.

                        SCHMID
          Put pressure on the wound.

                        EVERSMANN
          Yeah. It's gonna be all right, it's
          gonna be okay.

EXT. SLUM ALLEYS - NIGHT

Hoot, Sizemore and the Delta men move almost silently,
wearing NODS through the narrow alleyways.

Up ahead they see Durant's downed Black Hawk, figures
swarming over it, dragging off equipment. Hoot comes
charging up, firing over their heads:

                        HOOT
                  (in Somali, subtitled)
          I think this is mine!

The crowd bolts out of the Black Hawk and down the street.

                                              (CONTINUED)

CONTINUED:

INT. DURANT'S BLACK HAWK - LATER

No crew inside. Everything that can be ripped from the
control panel is gone.

Hoot sees Gordon's plastic pro-tech helmet, neat hole in the
forehead. Hoot picks it up and holds it for a moment, then
sets it on the console. Stares up at the men, eyes speaking
volumes.

They run from the wreckage and trigger a thermite charge in
the Black Hawk. As they run away, Super Six—Four EXPLODES,
thermite charge lighting up the sky.

INT. JOC - SAME TIME

The explosion flares on a screen. Garrison and others know
what it means. Their heads aren't bowed, but the atmosphere
in the room is like a funereal. A soldier hands Garrison a
radio.

                    GARRISON
          Cribbs?

INTERCUT TO EXT. OLYMPIC STADIUM - SAME TIME

SUPER: SAFE ZONE - PAKISTANI STADIUM

10TH MOUNTAIN AND U.N. BASE

                    CRIBBS
          Sir, they're still debating the route.

                    GARRISON (V.O.)
          How long?

                    CRIBBS
          At least a couple of hours.

                    GARRISON
          We haven't got that long, Joe.

The rescue convoy is assembling within an enormous soccer
stadium. Pakistani tanks pass Cribbs, who is on the phone as
his Little Bird flies over behind him.

                    CRIBBS
          Pakistani General said since we didn't
          deem to inform him of the raid, he's
          gonna take as much time as he wants.

                                        (CONTINUED)

CONTINUED:

> GARRISON
> (rubs his forehead)
> Well you tell the General this: I
> understand. But it is my duty to remind
> him that my men are surrounded by
> thousands of armed Somali militia. It is
> imperative that we move them out of the
> hostile area and into the safe zone. I
> need his help, now.

> CRIBBS
> Yes sir.

INT. HOUSE — NIGHT

Durant comes to in a room, lying on a paper-thin mattress,
back propped against the wall. Sees Firimbi, the man from
the crash site with the megaphone, stepping forward. He
holds Durant's dog tags.

> FIRIMBI
> Durant. Michael Durant.

> DURANT
> Yes.

> FIRIMBI
> You are the Ranger who kills my people?

Durant shakes his head no.

> DURANT
> I'm not a Ranger. I'm a pilot.

Firimbi offers Durant a cigarette. Durant shakes his head.

> FIRIMBI
> Huh. That's right. None of you
> Americans smoke anymore. You all live
> long, dull, uninteresting lives.

Durant tries to move, winces in pain.

> DURANT
> What do you want with me?

> FIRIMBI
> You have taken hostages. We have you.

> DURAN
> My government will never negotiate for
> me.

CONTINUED:

                    FIRIMBI
                (smiles)
          Then perhaps, you and I can negotiate.
          Huh? Soldier to soldier...hmm?

Firimbi offers Durant a drink. Durant shakes his head no.

                    DURANT
          I'm not in charge.

                    FIRIMBI
          Course not, you have the power to kill,
          but not negotiate. In Somalia, killing
          is negotiation. Do you really think if
          you get General Aidid, we will simply put
          down our weapons and adopt American
          Democracy? That the killing will stop?
          We know this: without victory there can
          be no peace. There will always be
          killing, you see? This is how things are
          in our world.

Firimbi tosses Durant his tags and walks out.

INT. MOGADISHU - NIGHT

A Black Hawk flies over the city.

INT. EVERSMANN'S POSITION - NIGHT

Eversmann watches Schmid work on Smith.

                    SCHMID
          You gotta take over for me. Both hands.

Schmid pulls Eversmann aside.

                    SCHMID (CONT'D)
          It's the femora artery. I can't see it.
          Which means that it's retracted up into
          the pelvis. Which means that I have to
          find it and clamp it. It's the only way
          to stop the bleeding... I got no more
          IV's. So, I'm gonna need you to assist.
          Okay?

                    EVERSMANN
          Yeah, yeah.

INT. EVERSMANN'S POSITION - MOMENTS LATER

CLOSE - on a pair of medical clamps. Eversmann holds the
clamps, he and Doc Schmid kneeling beside Smith.

                                        (CONTINUED)

CONTINUED:

                    SCHMID
          Now listen Jamie, I've gotta do
          something, it's going to hurt. Okay? I
          gotta cause you more pain, but I have to
          do it to help you. All right? You
          understand?

                    SMITH
          Give me some morphine.

                    SCHMID
          I can't. It'll lower your heart rate too
          far. I'm sorry. Here Twombly, why don't
          you take his hands there.

He's already hooked up to two IV bags, needles in both arms.

                    SCHMID (CONT'D)
          I need you to hold the wound open, keep
          pressure on the top of the leg. Yurek,
          you're gonna take the feet and the
          flashlight. On my count. All right,
          Jamie. All right man.

Schmid looks at Eversmann to ask, ready? Eversmann nods.

                    SCHMID (CONT'D)
          One, two, three.

Schmid pulls out the Curlex, releasing the blood flow, then
sticks both hands into the wound and probes for the artery.
Smith wails. Schmid probes around until --

                    SCHMID (CONT'D)
          Wait, wait, wait. Okay. I feel it. I
          feel the pulse.

                    EVERSMANN
          Yeah?

                    SCHMID
          I got it, I got it, I got it, yeah, I got
          it. I got it, I got it.

                    EVERSMANN
          You got it? You need these?

                    SCHMID
          Yeah, yeah. Clamp.

                    EVERSMANN
          Yeah, I got it clamped, I got it clamped.

                                        (CONTINUED)

                         SCHMID
          You got it? You got it? Hold it.

                         EVERSMANN
          Here, grab it. It's tearing.

Schmid pulls the slippery artery into the open. Eversmann
holds the clamp out, but the artery slithers away with a
snap.

                         SCHMID
          Fuck!

                         EVERSMANN
          It's going back in, it's going back in,
          it's tearing!

                         SCHMID
          Hold it! Fuck, okay get out, get out!

                         EVERSMANN
          Okay.

                         SCHMID
          Hold the wound.

                         EVERSMANN
          Okay, okay, I'm holding.

                         SCHMID
          Fuck!

                         SCHMID (CONT'D)
          Move your hand.

                         EVERSMANN
          Yeah.

Schmid's hands disappear into the wound again.

Gets the clamp ready, but Schmid can't locate the artery, he
shaking his head in frustration.

                         EVERSMANN (CONT'D)
          What?

Smith is passing out. Schmid has to give up the search
before he kills him. His bloody hands come out without the
artery. Angry at himself, he stuffs new Curlex into the
wound. Smith's eyes slit open as he weakly manages:

                         SMITH
          You fix it?

                                              (CONTINUED)

CONTINUED: (3)

The unused clamp is still in Eversmann's hand.

                    EVERSMANN
          Yeah, man. We got it.

Smith nods, eyes closing, passing out.

INT. ROOM - SANDERSON'S BUILDING - NIGHT

Grimes is grinding coffee beans.

                    SANDERSON
          What the hell are you doing?

                    GRIMES
          It's all in the grind, Sarge. Can't be
          too fine, can't be too coarse. Grimsey,
          you are squared away.

Grimes pours a cup of coffee.

EXT. DOWN THE STREET - NIGHT

Mo'Alim watches his men.

INT. ROOM - SANDERSON'S BUILDING - NIGHT

Grimes limps over to Sanderson who is sitting on a ratty
couch.

                    GRIMES
          Sarge, how'd you like a nice hot cup of
          Joe? Gold coast blend.

                    SANDERSON
          Sit down. Let me take a look at that
          foot.

                    GRIMES
          Oh no, it's not a problem.

                    SANDERSON
          Come on, come on, come on.

But Sanderson is already kneeling in front of him, cutting
off the laces Grimes's right boot.

Sanderson finishes cutting, slips the boot off to reveal -- a
golfball-sized piece of shrapnel sticking out of his foot.

                    SANDERSON (CONT'D)
          Oh.

                                        (CONTINUED)

CONTINUED:

                    GRIMES
          Oh my God. I don't even feel that.

                    SANDERSON
          It cauterized on impact.
               (wraps gauze around it)
          If this thing starts to smart, you let me
          know, all right? Where the hell'd they
          find you?

                    GRIMES
          Behind a desk.

Sanderson laughs.

                    GRIMES (CONT'D)
          No, really. You think I'm kidding?

BA-WHOOM! A blast shakes the house, walls rocking.

                    SANDERSON
          Anybody hit?

EXT. DOWN THE STREET - NIGHT

Mo'Alim shouts at a militia man, who adjusts the angle and
drops another missile in -- PHWOMP it shoots skyward.

INT. EVERSMANN'S POSITION - NIGHT

Everyone hits the deck as the round whistles in. This time
the house is rocked nearly off its foundation. Part of a
wall collapses. Doc Schmid covers Smith with his body.

                    EVERSMANN
          You all right? Is everybody all right?

Schmid nods his head yes.

EXT. DOWN THE STREET - NIGHT

BEYOND THE MASSIVE CITY ARCHWAY, Mo'Alim is wearing Russian-
made Night Vision goggles. He directs two technicals with
mortars on back, instructing his men to change angles and
fire again.

INT. EVERSMANN'S POSITION - NIGHT

The walls shake as another round comes in. Eversmann runs
forward.

                    EVERSMANN
          Incoming!

EXT. DOWN THE STREET - NIGHT

Mo'Alim fires an automatic weapon.

                MO'ALIM
           (in Somali, subtitled)
       Keep firing....faster!

EXT. DARKENED STREETS - NIGHT

Hoot, Sizemore and one other Delta man move slowly, silently
through the night, NODS on their heads. The sound of
staccato gunfire grows louder as they near Crash Site One.

A RUMBLE — and Hoot motions with hand signals. They creep
forward down the block, guns raised, NODs over their eyes.
They fire again -- and commandeer an RPG gun.

Mo'Alim looks around, as -- CRACK!CRACK! Two more militia -
drop to the ground. He sees Hoot load a mortar and fire it
directly at him.

Mo'Alim's head rocks backwards. He is dead.

Hoot, Sizemore and two Deltas run forward down the street.

EXT. OUTSIDE EVERSMANN'S POSITION - NIGHT

                HOOT
      Ranger here. This is Kilo One One.

INTERCUT to Galentine -

Galentine radios back:

              GALENTINE
      This is Chalk Four, we're at the
      Southeast corner of crash site. Who is
      this over?

                HOOT
      We're coming in with three friendlies. I
      need some covering fire, over.

GALENTINE - passes the word along, trying not to shout:

              GALENTINE
      Roger that Kilo One One. Hold your fire!
      Deltas coming in.

              SOLDIERS
        (in unison)
      Hold your fire!

(CONTINUED)

CONTINUED:

ON HOOT - down the block, Sizemore and Delta behind, the group moving in a rapid crouch, blending with shadows.

Rapid footsteps. Then the Rangers and the Delta Operators appearing in the night.

INT. JOC — LATER

Garrison looks at the screens. Says to a man behind him:

> GARRISON
> Ground personnel will have to mark target positions with infrared strobes. Get Little Birds on strafing runs and keep 'em going all night long.
> (stares at the monitors)
> If we don't hold back this city, we'll have a hundred caskets to fill by morning.

> OPERATOR
> Yes sir. Colonel Harrell, ground personnel at Crash Site One will have to mark the target with infrared strobes in preparation for air strike.

EXT. OLYMPIC STADIUM - NIGHT

As the complex logistics of organizing the vehicle Rescue Convoy continues --

McKnight, Struecker, Othic, and a group of Delta Operators arrive in jeeps. All are blood spattered or wounded from the ride through hell in the Humvee convoys.

Cribbs approaches as they climb out of the jeeps. Even Thomas, who didn't want to go before, is with them.

> CRIBBS
> McKnight! Between the tenth Mountain and U.N., we got enough personnel, okay? Danny, you guys do not have to go back out again.

McKnight looks at Cribbs.

> CRIBBS (CONT'D)
> All right, come on.

EXT. OLYMPIC STADIUM - LATER

The Rescue Convoy, finally, is about to leave. Humvees, trucks, tanks, and APCs.

(CONTINUED)

CONTINUED:

The tank treads grind and begin moving out, followed by the rest of the trucks.

SUPER: 11:23 PM

INT. EVERSMANN'S POSITION - NIGHT

It's been some time now.

                    SMITH
        I can't die here man.

                    EVERSMANN
        You're not gonna die, all right? You're
        not gonna die.

Eversmann is kneeling next to Doc Schmid and Smith. Eversmann is watching Smith, pale white, eyes glazed.

He says quietly to Eversmann:

                    SMITH
        I'm sorry.

                    EVERSMANN
        You don't have anything to be sorry for.
        You saved Twombly. You did perfect.

                    SMITH
            (eyes move to Twombly)
        You okay, Twombs?

Twombly has wandered over, stares down at Smith. Doesn't know what to say. Eversmann looks from Twombly to Smith.

                    TWOMBLY
        Yeah, I'm okay, Jamie.

Now the whole room is watching as Smith begins hyper-ventilating, a sickening wheezing sound echoing off the stone walls. Smith's eyes start to dart around the room.

                    EVERSMANN
        You did what you were trained to do. You
        should be proud of that. Be proud of
        that.

Smith nods, teeth chattering.

                    SMITH
      Ev?

CONTINUED:

                    EVERSMANN
Yeah?

                    SMITH
Do me a favor.

                    EVERSMANN
Yeah?

                    SMITH
You tell my parents, that I fought well
today. That I... that I... that I fought
hard.

                    EVERSMANN
You're gonna tell 'em yourself, okay?
You hear me?

Smith is shaking uncontrollably.

                    EVERSMANN (CONT'D)
All right?

                    SMITH
Are the Humvees here?

                    EVERSMANN
They're coming, Jamie.

                    SMITH
They're coming.

                    EVERSMANN
You just gotta hang in there a little
bit. You gotta hold out for just a
little bit, you can do that.

                    SMITH
I can.
        (gasping for breath)
I can do it. This is nothin'.

                    EVERSMANN
This is nothin'. It's nothin'.

                    SMITH
This is nothin'.

                    EVERSMANN
It's nothin'.

                    SMITH
Okay. Nothin'.

CONTINUED: (2)

Smith grips Eversmann's bloodstained hand. Eversmann nods.

                    EVERSMANN
          This is nothin'...

Smith's eyes begin to change...a certainty comes into them.
Now he stares somewhere beyond the ceiling -

Schmid runs forward.

                    SCHMID
          Oh shit! Hold the wound!

The Alamo house is silent, everyone watching as Schmid
administers CPR. Compresses Smith's chest again and again.

After a long time, Eversmann reaches out, stops Schmid.

Doc sits back, covered in blood. Stares down at Smith,
resigned.

                    EVERSMANN
          Oh, God.

INT. EVERSMANN'S POSITION — LATER

Slumped against a crumbling wall in the silent house,
Eversmann stares at Smith's body, covered by a tattered
blanket in the center of the room.

Hoot moves to the body, finds Smith's CAR-15 on the ground,
blood-spattered. Hoot picks it up, takes out the magazine.

                    EVERSMANN
          What are you doing?

Hoot doesn't look up as he clicks the rounds out one by one.

                    HOOT
          We need the ammo.

Eversmann watches the Delta soldier pick up the extra rounds.

                    HOOT (CONT'D)
          You did all you could here.

Eversmann's gaze again falls to Smith's form under the
blanket.

                    EVERSMANN
          They should've sent a medivac.

                                        (CONTINUED)

CONTINUED:

                    HOOT
          Well, right now we'd be out there
          defending another crashed chopper. More
          men would get torn up.

                    EVERSMANN
          Maybe...

Hoot walks over to the wall next to Eversmann.

                    HOOT
          So you're thinking. Don't.
               (beat)
          Cause Sergeant, you can't control who
          gets hit, or who doesn't. Who falls out
          of a chopper, or why. It ain't up to
          you. It's just war.

                    EVERSMANN
               (nods, he knows, but)
          Smith is still dead. If Blackburn
          wouldn't fallen none of this woulda
          happened --

                    HOOT
               (stares at him)
          Listen -- should have or could have -- it
          don't matter; You'll get plenty of time
          to think about all that later.
          Believe me.

Hoot looks at Eversmann.

                    HOOT (CONT'D)
          Sergeant. You got your men this far.
          You did it right today...
               (Eversmann glances up at him)
          You need to start thinking about getting
          these men out of here.

Hoot looks up.

                    HOOT (CONT'D)
          Well, shall we?

INT. EVERSMANN'S POSITION - LATER

Gunfire erupts around them. The men rush out to defend their
position.

                    EVERSMANN
          I need four guns on this corner, now!

INT./EXT. WOOD'S LITTLE BIRD / CHASE SITE — NIGHT

As Wood brings the Little Bird in low, there are suddenly
countless dots of light surrounding the entire perimeter of
the area, from the streets and rooftops ringing the court
yard — all firing at him.

He sees THOUSANDS of glowing Somali bodies, ghostly,
innumerable on his infra—red monitor.

ADJOINING ROOFTOPS - more than two-hundred beat signatures of
Somali bodies charge across rooftops, coming toward the
chalks in a great wave, leaping from roof to roof.

OPPOSITE SIDE OF THE STREET - three hundred Somalis move to
get in position to fire down at the chalks. Somalis climb up
staircases, ladders, appearing on rooftops like angry
insects.

                    WOOD
          Jesus Christ! Look at that.

Wood pilots a nimble Little Bird over the crash site. Sees
nothing but dark forms around buildings and a blur of wrecked
metal below as he shrieks past.

INTERCUT to Eversmann -

                    EVERSMANN
          This is Two Five. I can see you, you're
          right above me.

                    WOOD
          Eversmann, I can't tell who's who down
          there. Too much activity.

INT. JOINT OPERATIONS CENTER - CONT.

ON A MONITOR - infrared figures of Rangers hiding in
buildings around the crash site illuminate the video screens:
white blobs, like something out of a low—tech video game.

INTERCUT to Eversmann -

                    EVERSMANN
          I'll mark the target with a strobe, over?

                    WOOD
          Roger that.

EXT. EVERSMANN'S POSITION - NIGHT

Eversmann throws a strobe. It does not fire.

INT. WOOD'S LITTLE BIRD - SAME TIME

Wood looks for the strobe to flash.

>   EVERSMANN (V.O.)
>   See it?

>   WOOD
>   Nah, I can't see shit.

INTERCUT to Eversmann -

Eversmann is at the radio, Galentine shaking his bead, no.

>   EVERSMANN
>   I'm puttin' it on the roof.

Eversmann begins gathering the IR strobes. Hoot says:

>   HOOT
>   You're gonna need some help.

>   EVERSMANN
>   Cover me.

>   HOOT
>   Okay guys, we're gonna lay down some
>   cover fire for him on three. Ready?
>   One, two, three, go!

His chalk finishes reloading and sets to cover him. He looks
at them. Ready? Is he? Yes. Whup-whup-whup -- Wood's
Little Bird howls overhead. Somalis FIRING as --

EXT. CRASH SITE - NIGHT

-- Eversmann sprints from the Somali building into the
shooting range of the street, bullets tracking him -- a
hellstorm, Eversmann right in the middle of it.

Eversmann tosses the strobe on the roof.

INT. WOOD'S LITTLE BIRD

Wood sees the strobe flash through his NOD.

>   WOOD
>   I got your position, I got the target.
>   We're inbound and hot.

RPG explode outside the bird, lighting up the sky and rocking
the craft. Wood hits the trigger on the flight stick.

(CONTINUED)

CONTINUED:

His miniguns blaze strobelight—death across the rooftops.
Somali heat signatures scatter under the withering fire of
the swift chopper's deadly arsenal.

EVERSMANN - Finished, prepares for the final run back to the
Alamo building.

The street echoes with the roar of weapons as Eversmann leaps
inside to safety.

Figures fire their weapons down the block toward the crash
site.

The Little Birds turn to make another pass.

                    WOOD (CONT'D)
          Ya'll keep your heads down. We're coming
          back around.

INT. JOC - SAME TIME

Garrison watches the screen. Steele's voice comes in through
the radio.

INT. STEELE'S STABLE COURTYARD - NIGHT

Steele radios in -

                    STEELE
          Six Two, this is Six Four. Where the
          hell's the convoy? Over.

                    HARRELL (V.O.)
          Half a block from your location, hang in
          there.

EXT. EVERSMANN'S POSITION - NIGHT

An RPG slams into the wall, rocking the building.

                    EVERSMANN
          Shit!

The Little Bird again shrieks past his building, miniguns
rumbling.

Bullets ZING over their heads, blasting walls inside the
house. Somali fire increases, web tightening. Chalk Four
returns fire, guns raging through the night.

Thousands of muzzle flashes rain from rooftops, windows and
doorways of the buildings across the street. Somali bullets
SMACK! and CRACK! all around them.

INT. JOC - SAME TIME

Wood's voice comes over the command net.

>   WOOD (V.O.)
>   C2, miniguns dry. Returning to base.

>   COLONEL MATTHEWS (V.O.)
>   Roger that. Second team inbound. Your
>   station. On your location, four minutes.

ON SCREEN - as the chopper passes, smoke rises from the crash
site.

INT. STEELE'S POSITION - LATER

THE RESCUE CONVOY - rumbling down the block. .50 cals
roaring from atop Humvees. Somalis are blown back into
buildings by the dozen.

The massive convoy reduces Somali positions into dust, entire
buildings crumbling like saltine crackers. Dark figures
continue to fall. Somali muzzle flashes dissipate...

Captain Steele steps from the stable doorway and shakes hands
with Colonel McKnight.

>   CAPTAIN STEELE
>   Captain Steele here, Colonel!

>   MCKNIGHT
>   Get your men loaded up Captain. We're
>   gettin' the hell outta here.

>   CAPTAIN STEELE
>   Yes, sir! All right, let's go. Be
>   careful with the wounded.

Steele grabs the radio:

>   STEELE
>   Two Five, this is Six Four, the rescue
>   column has arrived and will be at your
>   location in about ten minutes. Prepare
>   your men for exfil Sergeant.

INT. EVERSMANN'S POSITION - NIGHT

Eversmann closes his eyes and nods.

>   STEELE (V.O.)
>   Six Four out.

(CONTINUED)

CONTINUED:

                         EVERSMANN
          Yeah, Roger that, sir. Roger that!

                         STEELE (V.O.)
          All right, let's move it!

                         EVERSMANN
          Ten minutes! The convoy's gonna be here
          in ten minutes!

His Rangers breathe a collective sigh of relief.

INT. EVERSMANN'S POSITION - LATER

Kurth, Waddell, and Galentine are covering their position,
weapons aimed out the doorway and firing into the night.

                         KURTH
          Eversmann, I'm out!

                         EVERSMANN
          This is my last one!

SUPER: 02:05 AM

Eversmann goes to the door and stares at the incredible sight
of the convoy, so long he can't see the end of it. He shouts
over his shoulder:

                         EVERSMANN (CONT'D)
          The convoy's here!

Random gunfire that comes from Somali houses are met with the
full wrath of the U.S. Mountain Division as --

Eversmann sees McKnight striding alongside the lead Humvee,
ignoring random Somali gunfire as if it doesn't exist.

                         MCKNIGHT
          Sergeant Eversmann?

                         EVERSMANN
          Yes, sir!

McKnight sees him in the darkness. Walks toward him, hand
outstretched.

                         MCKNIGHT
          Heard you guys needed a lift.

                         EVERSMANN
              (can't help smiling)
          Yes, sir.

                                             (CONTINUED)

CONTINUED:

And he shakes the Colonel's outstretched hand.

                    MCKNIGHT
          Bring you wounded right over there!

INT. WOLCOTT'S BLACK HAWK - DAWN

A Ranger takes a saw and cuts through the metal of Wolcott's
Black Hawk.

EXT. SANDERSON'S POSITION - NIGHT

Sanderson watches Grimes hobble to the doorway and goes to
assist.

                    SANDERSON
          Hey, I got ya!

Grimes smiles through the pain, hobbling on his bad foot
toward the waiting APC.

                    GRIMES
          It's okay. I wanna walk.

                    SANDERSON
               (lets Grimes go)
          You sure? Go!

Sanderson watches Grimes run into the APC under his own
power.

EXT. WOLCOTT'S BLACK HAWK — NIGHT

The saws are still at work.

EXT. EVERSMANN'S POSITION   NIGHT

Eversmann and Doc Schmid carry Smith's body, covered with a
sheet, out into the night. Load it into an APC. Hoot covers
them, watching the rooftops, windows. Ever vigilant.

EXT. WOLCOTT'S BLACK HAWK — NIGHT

                    RANGER
          I got him. One, two, three.

Wilkinson and Fales are helped by dozens of Rangers as they
carefully pass the wounded Warren and Dowdy out of the ruined
helicopter.

INT. LEAD APC - NIGHT

Cribbs speaks to the Pakistani drivers.

                                        (CONTINUED)

CONTINUED:

                        CRIBBS
        Get the pilots' bodies out, then we go to
        the stadium.

Behind Cribbs, soldiers load the many wounded and dead into
vehicles. Groaning men are piled onto one another in the
cramped APCs. Humvees are packed full.

NEAR THE FOUNTAIN: Cribbs walks up to McKnight, Steele,
Eversmann, Hoot and SANDERSON.

                  CRIBBS (CONT'D)
        We're running out of room already.

                  MCKNIGHT
        We're just gonna have to cram 'em in to
        every possible space.

                      CRIBBS
        Okay. Tenth Mountain will provide
        security for armor, walks us out of the
        hot zone --

                    STEELE
         (disdain on his face)
        Tenth Mountain? No, Sir, with respect,
        my Rangers can provide rear security.
        We'll walk you out of the hot zone, and
        then we'll jump on the last few vehicles.

Cribbs looks at the battle weary faces before him.

                      CRIBBS
        Okay, let's get out of here.

                    STEELE
        Let's go!

INT. APC - DAWN

Inside the coffin-like APC, Grimes pounds on the driver's
partition as bullets PING off the metal hull.

                    GRIMES
        Come on! These things are fucking bullet
        magnets! Come on, let's go!

                PAKISTANI DRIVER
        We go when I'm ordered to, soldier.

.. WOLCOTT'S BLACK HAWK - DAWN

They start on Wolcott.

> RANGER
> Easy, go easy. Easy. Go easy.

A Ranger shines a light on Wolcott's buried legs. It's hopeless.

INT. JOC - DAY

He stares at the screen. Garrison can see Somalis again massing around three streets, choking off the convoy's exits.

> GARRISON
> Colonel, what is going on down there?

INTERCUT to McKnight on radio --

> MCKNIGHT
> They're dismantling the entire cockpit around the body.

> GARRISON (V.O.)
> Well how long's it gonna take? I need an honest, no shit assessment.

There's a pause as McKnight relays the question. Then --

> MCKNIGHT
> They can't say.

INTERCUT to Garrison. He endures as long as he can the flares on the screen he knows are RPGS. Eventually, into his mic -

> GARRISON
> Danny, no one gets left behind.

INTERCUT to McKnight --

> GARRISON (V.O.) (CONT'D)
> You understand me, son?

INTERCUT to McKnight. No response.

> GARRISON (CONT'D)
> Danny?

INTERCUT to Garrison. Finally --

(CONTINUED)

CONTINUED:

                        MCKNIGHT (V.O.)
             Yes, General.

                        GARRISON
             You do what you have to do.

                        MCKNIGHT
             Roger.

EXT. WOLCOTT'S BLACK HAWK - MORNING

Briley's body is carried away from the Black Hawk

SUPER: 5:45 A.M. - Monday, October 4

Gunfire rains down on the men.

                        MCKNIGHT
             Let's go! Let's move out!

The convoy starts to roll out. Rangers follow on foot.

EXT. WOLCOTT'S BLACK HAWK - SAME TIME

Hoot sets explosives in the now-deserted cockpit. Runs to
the leaving convoy as the charges are detonated.

EXT. CHASE SITE - DAWN

The convoy is picking up speed, the Mountain soldiers
scrambling to get aboard Humvees and APCs as Eversmann,
Sanderson, and the other Rangers and Delta cover them.

EXT. CRASH SITE - DAWN

After the last of the APCs pass, Eversmann and the other
Rangers and Delta try to get aboard. EVERY VEHICLE is
crammed full, some men hanging out open doors, some lying on
hoods.

No one stops for them. Steele runs alongside the APC,
pounding on the metal --

                        STEELE
             Open up the hatch! We got men back here!

                        PAKISTANI DRIVER
             No room here, go on the roof.

                        SANDERSON
             What's going on?

                                            (CONTINUED)

CONTINUED:

                    STEELE
          The roof?

                    TWOMBLY
          I'm not getting on the fucking roof!

                    SANDERSON
          No, no, no, it's full!

The Pakistani driver shouts.

Steele shuts the door. There are no more vehicles to chase
after.

                    SANDERSON (CONT'D)
          Let's just go, let's just go!

The convoy pulls out and the men follow on foot.

EXT. BACK AT THE SOMALI BUILDING - DAWN

The city is bathed in orange light. Eversmann, Hoot, Steele,
Sanderson, Twombly, Sizemore, Nelson, Yurek, Kurth, Waddell,
Galentine and Doc Schmid are running down the streets after
the convoy, unable to catch up with the vehicles.

They watch helplessly as the convoy disappears down the
block. Their tired, rubbery legs carry them away from the
crash site, into the dense, dangerous streets of surrounding
neighborhoods.

EXT. MOGADISHU STREETS - MORNING

The group of soldiers are now running along the same streets
they battled over the day before.

The men are exhausted, gasping for air as they charge down
the crooked, dirty roads. Legs like lead weights.

KRATAKRATAKRAT! Machine-gun fire rakes the road ahead. The
group runs for cover, trying not to get pinned in.

EXT. K-4 CIRCLE - MORNING

The Rescue Convoy rumbles, stretching back a quarter mile.
The sound of the vehicles shakes the very earth. An older
Somali man carries a dead child and crosses in front of the
convoy.

EXT. MOGADISHU STREETS - MORNING

The group runs down the street. Gasping. They can see the
convoy disappearing around a corner.

                                             (CONTINUED)

CONTINUED:

Sanderson and Hoot FIRE down the intersection, killing three
Somali snipers. Steele, Eversmann and others charge across.

On the other side, the Rangers cover Delta Hoot and
Sanderson.

The Delta Operators charge across to safety.

They use this tactic at every intersection. Somali gunfire
getting more intense. The men see the APCs, distant blocks
ahead, rounding a corner.

EXT. THE CORNER - MORNING

Sanderson charges up from behind, bullets following him.

THEY RUN out into the street as -- A WOMAN with a child in
her arms dashes out in front of them, hurrying across the
street. Waddell almost fires on instinct.

                    WADDELL
          Get down, get outta here!

The woman runs to the other side of the street.

Sanderson runs over to Eversmann.

                    EVERSMANN
          I'm out of ammo! Sanderson, I'm out of
          ammo!

Sanderson continues to fire.

Another woman runs forward, Kurth raises his weapon to fire.

                    YUREK
          What are you doing?

                    KURTH
          I'm doing it.

The woman RAISES A HANDGUN -- Kurth fires and she falls dead.

EXT. MOGADISHU STREETS - MORNING

The group runs down the street, bullets whizzing past.

The men charge down the block on wobbly legs, running through
the smoke. People line the streets, cheering them on.

They run into the safety of THE SOCCER STADIUM.

INT. OLYMPIC STADIUM

The entrance is in sight. Doctors are inside, white tables
and sheets and water and safety and food and shelter and -
Eversmann makes it. Hoot, Sanderson, Steele, and the others
charge in after him.

They stare at the makeshift medical tents that have been set
up. Watching a Medic directing the seriously wounded to one
area, dead to another -

- as UN workers bring them glasses of water.

Nelson and Twombly embrace.

Eversmann staggers forward.

EXT. STADIUM — MORNING

BEHIND THEM — Colonel McKnight gets his neck wound looked at.

                    MCKNIGHT
          Ah, shit.

                    MEDIC
          The bullet missed your jugular by about
          three millimeters. Don't move!

                    MCKNIGHT
          All right, all right. Hurry up, hurry
          up!

BEHIND HIM - Grimes, covered in white dust, rests on a
litter. Sanderson walks over to him and hands him a cup.

                    GRIMES
          Little short on coffee, but I got you
          some tea. How you doing soldier?

                    RANGER
          I can't feel a thing.

INT. THE MEDICAL WARD - OPERATING ROOM - DAY

Garrison, standing by the door, has come into the chaos that
is the medical tent, watching. Somebody shouts, "...mop..."
And we see doctors and medics working over a man, the man
bleeding profusely, the doctors and the medics literally
slipping in his blood on the floor... And Garrison seeing a
mop nearby takes it up, and doing his duty, mops the bloody
floor... And as Garrison mops the bloody floor the doctors
and the medics are trying to save his men's lives...

INT. THE MEDICAL WARD - LATER

Steele moves through the tent... men in various conditions...
none of it good... He comes to Ruiz. The medic shakes his
head no.

                    STEELE
          Hey son, hey.

Ruiz opens his eyes.

                    RUIZ
          Captain.

                    STEELE
          Lorenzo? How're you doing?

                    RUIZ
          I went in and out. Medic says I should
          be okay in a couple of days.

                    STEELE
          That's great news.

                    RUIZ
          Are we going after them?

                    STEELE
          You bet your ass we will. We gotta
          regroup.

                    RUIZ
          Don't go out there without me. Don't go
          back out there without me. I can still
          do my job.

Steele puts his hand on Ruiz' face.

                    STEELE
          Now you get some rest now.

EXT. STADIUM — MORNING

Eversmann comes over to Hoot, who is picking through
supplies... resupplying himself. Hoot goes about his
business... taping grenade pins one after another after
another... Calmly, efficiently...

                    EVERSMANN
                (incredibly)
          You're going back in?

                                        (CONTINUED)

CONTINUED:

                    HOOT
           (nods, matter of fact)
    There's still men out there...God damn!

He stops resupplying and picks up a plate and eats.

                HOOT (CONT'D)
    When I go home...and people ask me, hey
    Hoot? Why do you do it man? Why? You
    some kind of war junkie? I won't say a
    god damned word. Why? Because they
    won't understand... They won't understand
    why we do it. They won't understand,
    it's about the men next to you...and
    that's it... that's all it is.

Eversmann does know...and starts to resupply himself. Hoot
shakes his head no.

                HOOT (CONT'D)
    Hey. Don't even think about it, all
    right? I'm better on my own.

And fully resupplied Hoot simply starts off... Eversmann
watches Hoot walk away... And Hoot suddenly slows,
realizing... shouting back...

                HOOT (CONT'D)
           (congratulations)
    Hey! We started a whole new week...it's
    Monday.

And as he moves off... just another soldier, one of the dog's
of war...

EXT. WOLCOTT'S BLACK HAWK - DAY

Kids play on the downed helicopter.

                EVERSMANN (V.O.)
    I was talking to Blackburn the other day,
    and he asked me, "You know what changed?
    Why are we going home?" And I said,
    "Nothing..." But that's not true, you
    know? I think everything's changed. I
    know I've changed...

INT. A STORAGE ROOM - LATE DAY

Fluorescent lights. . .too bright.. .too constant... a
cooler's humming...it kicks off and then on again...and we
see EVERSMANN...And he's clean...just some nicks and cuts,
band-aid pieces over some small wounds...but there are other
wounds, the kind you can't see at first glance...a soldier
who's been in combat...a look in a young man's eyes... a look
that makes you stop and take a deeper look...into his
soul...and that's just what we do...looking at his
face...into his eyes...into the window of his soul...as he's
talking to someone...easy, conversational...nothing out of
the ordinary...

                    EVERSMANN
          You know, a friend of mine asked me
          before I got here, it was when we were
          all shipping out. He asked me ..."Why
          are you going to fight somebody else's
          war? What do ya'll think, you're
          heros...?"

He laughs at the idea...

                    EVERSMANN (CONT'D)
          I didn't know what to say at the time,
          but... if he asks me again...I'd
          say...No. I'd say there's no way in
          hell...nobody asks to be a hero...it just
          sometimes turns out that way...

And for the first time we see he's been talking to a familiar
man, lying motionless on a stretcher...

And Eversmann, needing to make a final connection touches
Smith's chest...a hero's heart...another somebody who didn't
ask to be a hero..

                    EVERSMANN (CONT'D)
               (simply)
          I'm gonna talk to your ma and pa when I
          get home, okay?

And we see there are other men on stretchers, other young men
who left a piece of their hearts behind..

And he turns and leaves...the lights forever on...the cooler
humming...the boys going home men...

INT. AIRPLANE CARGO BAY - LATE IN THE DAY

The cargo bay door closes on the empty cargo bay.

FADE TO BLACK...

LEGEND #1

During the raid over 1000 Somalis died and 19 American
soldiers lost their lives.

CWO Donovan Briley
Staff Sgt. Daniel Busch
Spec. James Cavaco
Staff Sgt. William Cleveland
Staff Sgt. Thomas Field
Sgt. First Class Earl Fillmore
CWO Raymond Frank
Master Sgt. Gary Gordon
Sgt. Cornell Houston
Sgt. Casey Joyce
Pfc. Richard Kowalewski
Pfc. James Martin
Master Sgt. Tim 'Griz' Martin
Sgt. Dominick Pilla
Sgt. First Class Matt Rierson
Sgt. Lorenzo Ruiz
Sgt. First Class Randy Shughart
Cpl. Jamie Smith
CWO Cliff 'Elvis' Wolcott

> RUIZ (V.O.)
> My love, you're strong and you'll do well
> in life. I love you and my children
> deeply. Today and tomorrow, with each
> day, grow and grow. Keep smiling and
> never give up, even when things get you
> down. So in closing my love, tonight,
> tuck my children in bed warmly. Tell
> them I love them. Then, hug them for me
> and, give them both a kiss good night for
> Daddy.

Legend #2

Delta Sgts. Gary Gordon and Randy Shughart were the first
soldiers to receive the medal of honor posthumously since the
Vietnam War.

Michael Durant was released after 11 days of captivity.

Two weeks later, President Clinton withdrew Delta Force and
The Rangers from Somalia.

(CONTINUED)

CONTINUED:

Legend #3

Major General William F. Garrison accepted full
responsibility for the outcome of the raid.

On August 2, 1996, Warlord Mohamed Farrah Aidid was killed in
Mogadishu. The following day, General Garrison retired.

STILLS AND STORYBOARDS

CHALK FOUR

JOSH HARTNETT
as Eversmann

EWAN MC GREGOR
as Grimes

ORLANDO BLOOM
as Blackburn

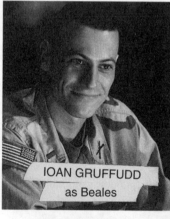

IOAN GRUFFUDD
as Beales

THOMAS HARDY
as Twombly

CHRIS BEETEM
as Joyce

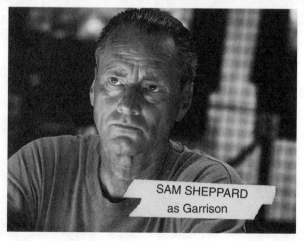

SAM SHEPPARD
as Garrison

CHALK FOUR

TOM SIZEMORE
as McKnight

CHARLIE HOFHEIMER
as Smith

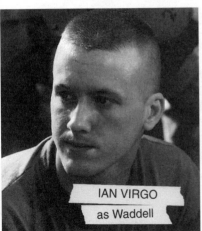

IAN VIRGO
as Waddell

GABRIEL CASSEUS
as Kurth

CARMINE GIOVINAZZO
as Goodale

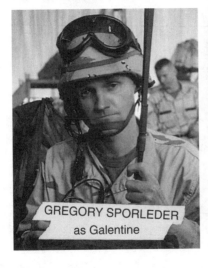

GREGORY SPORLEDER
as Galentine

THOMAS GUIRY
as Yurek

DELTA

ERIC BANA
as Hoot

WILLIAM FICHTNER
as Sanderson

NIKOLAJ COSTER-WALDAU
as Gordon

JOHNNY STRONG
as Shughart

KIM COATES
as Wex

RICHARD TYSON
as Busch

CONVOYS

JASON ISSACS
as Steele

BRIAN VAN HOLT
as Stuecker

MATTHEW MARSDEN
as Sizemore

ENRIQUE MURCIANO
as Ruiz

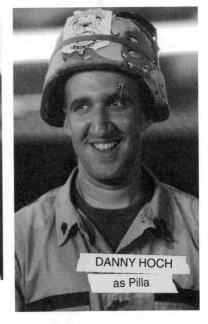

DANNY HOCH
as Pilla

Above: Josh Hartnett, as Sgt. Matt Eversmann, leads his chalk to an awaiting armada of Little Bird and Black Hawk choppers. **Below:** Sunday, October 3, 1993—Task Force Ranger thunders over the Somali coastline, preparing to sweep over the city of Mogadishu. **Right:** Sam Shepard as Maj. General Garrison watches the raid from the high-tech Joint Operations Center. *(Stills Captions by Ken Nolan)*

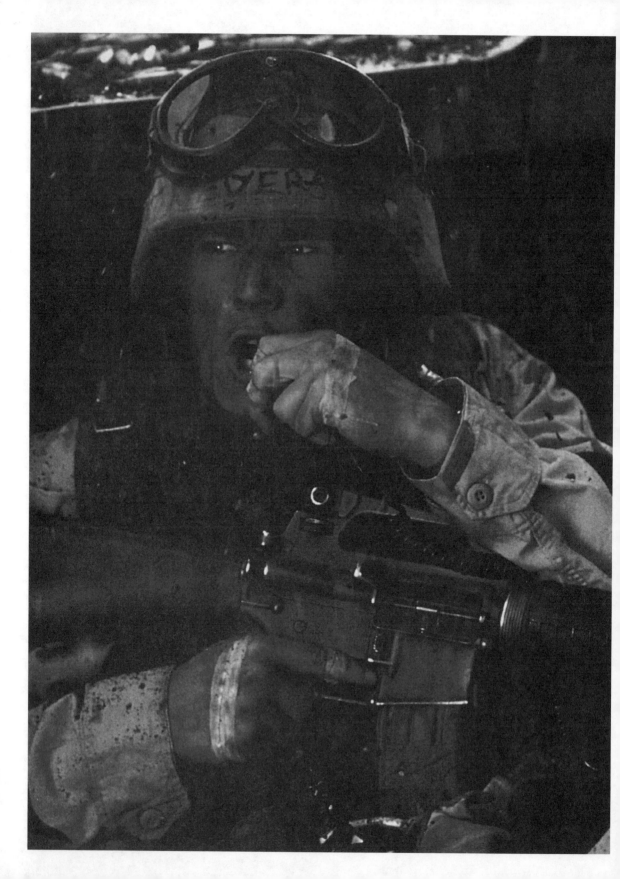

Left: "We've got a Black Hawk down!" Eversmann radios his superiors on the war-torn streets of Mogadishu. **Above:** Eversmann calls for help as Doc Schmid (Hugh Dancy) checks the vitals of Private Blackburn (Orlando Bloom). **Below:** "We need an immediate Medivac for a critical casualty." Eversmann and Galentine (Gregory Sporleder) request a medical chopper for the wounded Crpl. Smith (Charlie Hofheimer).

Above: Sgt. Yurek (Thomas Guiry) takes cover as bullets pierce the metal door of a cramped Somali schoolhouse. **Below:** Private Maddox (Michael Roof) surveys the carnage around him as he steps away from the "Lost Humvee Convoy." **Right:** "Go! Go!" Rangers fast-rope from a Black Hawk to the dangerous Mogadishu streets. **Following page:** 3:42 P.M., October 3, 1993—Delta "Operators," seated on side benches of AH-6 Little Bird helicopters, prepare to land on Hawlwadig Road to begin the mission.

Above: Director Ridley Scott and producer Jerry Bruckheimer discuss an upcoming scene on-set in Morocco. **Above right:** Shutterbugs: Producer Bruckheimer with his ever-present camera, and director Scott. **Below right:** "Action." Ridley Scott, a director of Zen-like calm and patience, surveys his domain.

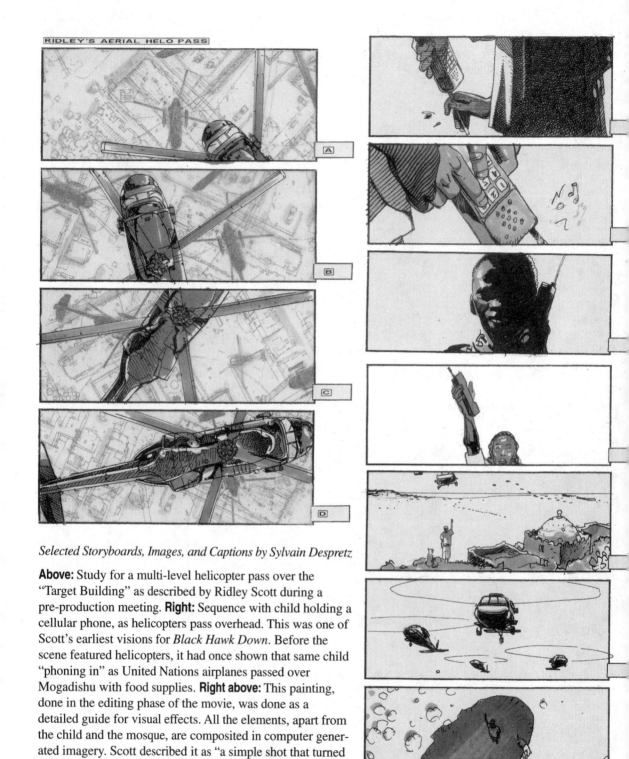

RIDLEY'S AERIAL HELO PASS

A

B

C

D

Selected Storyboards, Images, and Captions by Sylvain Despretz

Above: Study for a multi-level helicopter pass over the "Target Building" as described by Ridley Scott during a pre-production meeting. **Right:** Sequence with child holding a cellular phone, as helicopters pass overhead. This was one of Scott's earliest visions for *Black Hawk Down*. Before the scene featured helicopters, it had once shown that same child "phoning in" as United Nations airplanes passed over Mogadishu with food supplies. **Right above:** This painting, done in the editing phase of the movie, was done as a detailed guide for visual effects. All the elements, apart from the child and the mosque, are composited in computer generated imagery. Scott described it as "a simple shot that turned out to be the most problematic of the whole film."

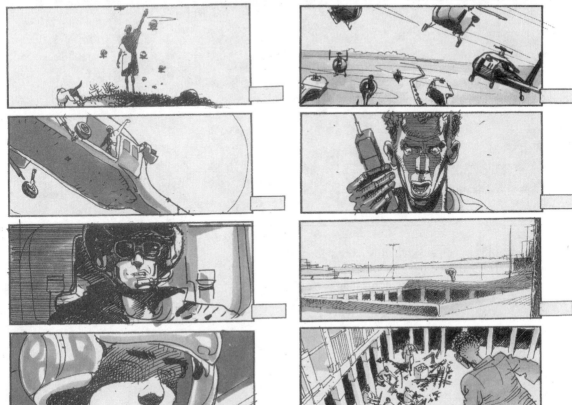

Top of page: First of half a dozen illustrations done at the request of Scott and Jerry Bruckheimer. These drawings went to the Pentagon, along with a presentation aimed at obtaining Army approval of the picture. **Above:** Matt Eversmann drags a fallen Todd Blackburn off the street and away from a rain of bullets. **Right:** Chalk Four lands at the target building. **Following page:** This top shot of the target building shows a dramatic view of the scene moments before everything goes wrong.

PRODUCTION NOTES

Leave No Man Behind:
The Making of *Black Hawk Down*

"The story of combat is timeless. It is about the same
things whether in Troy or Gettysburg, Normandy or
the Ia Drang. It is about soldiers, most of them young,
trapped in a fight to the death. The extreme and terrible
nature of war touches something essential about being
human...."

—Mark Bowden, *Black Hawk Down:*
A Story of Modern War

"Surrender is not a Ranger word. I will never leave a
fallen comrade to fall into the hands of the enemy..."
—From the "Ranger Creed"

From acclaimed director Ridley Scott and renowned producer Jerry
Bruckheimer, based on actual events, *Black Hawk Down* is the heroic account
of a group of elite U.S. soldiers sent into Mogadishu, Somalia, in October
1993 as part of a U.N. peacekeeping operation. Their mission: to capture
two top lieutenants of the Somali warlord, Mohamed Farrah Aidid, as part
of a strategy to quell the civil war and famine that are ravaging the country.

The U.S. troops come to Somalia with good intentions, hoping to save
lives, not take them. Increasingly mired in Somalia's incomprehensible feu-
dal politics—in which one clan has been pitted against another for a
millennium—the soldiers are destined for a brutal education when the
carefully planned mission takes unexpected turns... resulting in the U.S.
military's single biggest firefight since Vietnam.

When the mission commences, it appears every man, woman, and child
in Mogadishu takes up arms against the Americans, turning the city into a

deadly combat zone. And when two seemingly invincible Black Hawk heli-copters are shot down over the city, the mission abruptly changes into a desperate race against time to rescue the surviving flight crews and, finally, the soldiers on the ground. Young Rangers and veteran Delta Force soldiers must fight side by side against overwhelming odds. Outnumbered and sur-rounded for 18 harrowing hours, they remain trapped and wounded in the most hostile district of Mogadishu until a rescue convoy can retrieve them. Tensions flare, friends are lost, and alliances formed, and soldiers learn the true nature of war and heroism.

What happened on October 3, 1993, might ultimately have been a foot-note to history—but for the Americans who survived, that late afternoon's journey into night was to be the single defining moment of their lives.

For the U.S. soldiers who didn't, it was to be their epitaph, burned into the dusty streets of a helltorn African city most of them had never even heard of—an epitaph of bravery, commitment, and selflessness. *Black Hawk Down*—a story of combat at once epic and intimate—follows them step-by-step throughout the conflict on the ground, in the air, and at the command cen-ter. Much of the story is experienced through the eyes of Staff Sgt. Matt Eversmann (Josh Hartnett), an idealistic young Ranger whose mettle is sorely tested when he is unexpectedly handed command of one of the four "chalks" assigned to secure the target building. We also experience the event with a myriad other characters, portrayed by a large ensemble of newcomers and experienced actors from both sides of the Atlantic.

The Production Team

Ridley Scott, one of the most honored filmmakers of our time, teamed for the first time with Jerry Bruckheimer, one of the most successful producers ever, to bring *Black Hawk* to the screen. Their remarkable team of behind-the-camera artists includes director of photography Slawomir Idziak (*Proof of Life*, Krzysztof Kieslowski's *Dekalog* series), production designer Arthur Max (Academy Award® nominee and British Academy Award winner for *Gladiator*, who also collaborated with Ridley Scott on *G.I. Jane*), costume designers Sammy Howarth-Sheldon (assistant costume designer for *Gladiator*, which won the Oscar® in that category) and David Murphy (*Hamburger Hill*).

Film editor Pietro Scalia, A.C.E., was also an Oscar® nominee and British Academy Award winner for *Gladiator*, and won an Academy Award® for editing Oliver Stone's *JFK*. Composer Hans Zimmer created the heralded scores for both *Gladiator* and *Hannibal*, among many others. VFX Supervisor

152

Tim Burke and special effects supervisor Neil Courbould both won Academy Awards® for their work on *Gladiator*. The second unit director is Alexander Witt, who also worked on *Gladiator*, as well as on Jerry Bruckheimer's *Remember the Titans*.

The screenplay is by Ken Nolan, based on the bestselling book by Mark Bowden that explored, in great detail, the Battle of Mogadishu.

October 3, 1993: The Mission

It might have been relatively simple... if anything in war can be termed simple: a quick extraction from a target building in downtown Mogadishu of two lieutenants and other "Tier One" associates of brutal warlord Mohamed Farrah Aidid, leader of the Habr Gidr subclan, determined to maintain power over his increasingly anarchic country, even at the price of starving and killing his fellow Somalis. U.S. soldiers were in Somalia as part of a multinational United Nations force that was attempting to maintain some kind of peace and prevent the mass starvation that had erupted across the East African nation, killing some 300,000 people—partially from famine, partially because warlords such as Aidid were hoarding food provided by the peacekeepers and killing their own countrymen as they attempted to collect relief packages. One of the Habr Gidr clan's responses to the U.N. efforts was to ambush 24 Pakistani soldiers under the world body's flag and literally eviscerate them.

By capturing Aidid's lieutenants, the U.S. hoped to cut off the warlord at his feet, whittling away his power bit by bit. Thus, under the command of Gen. William F. Garrison, a mission was devised to capture the clan leaders who would be meeting in a house near the Olympic Hotel on Mogadishu's downtown Hawlwadig Road. About 75 U.S. Rangers in four separate chalks would fast-rope down from four Black Hawk helicopters to provide cover for a Delta assault force of about 40 men, which would storm the building, "extract" the targeted clan members, and bring them to a convoy of 12 Humvees and trucks that would travel up Hawlwadig to pick up the prisoners and return them to the U.S. base some three miles outside of the city near the Indian Ocean.

The mission was scheduled to begin at 3:42 in the afternoon and last, perhaps, 45 minutes to an hour. Night vision goggles and other special equipment were left back at the U.S. base three miles away near the Indian Ocean... they wouldn't be needed. But when Black Hawks Super Six One and then Super Six Four were shot down within 20 minutes of each other, the mission took a fateful turn from an assault into a rescue mission. The city was essentially a hornet's nest as American soldiers on the ground found themselves under heavy fire from well-armed Somali civilians. The battle that ensued would rage all through the night and into the morning of October 4, resulting in 18 Americans dead, 73 injured, and huge casualties among the Somalis, who waged furious war on soldiers who were perceived as enemies and invaders.

Mission Timeline

October 3, 1993

2:49 P.M. The principal targets, Habr Gidr clan leaders, are spotted at a building on Hawlwadig Road in downtown Mogadishu.

3:32 P.M. The force launches with 19 aircraft, 12 vehicles, and 160 men.

3:42 P.M. The assault begins, with four Ranger chalks fast-roping in from four hovering Black Hawk helicopters and Delta Force soldiers delivered on Little Bird choppers. One Ranger, Pvt. Todd Blackburn, misses the rope and falls some 60 feet to the street.

4:00 P.M. Forces of armed Somali militia converge on the target area from all over Mogadishu.

4:02 P.M. Assault forces report both clan leaders and about 21 others in custody. As the force prepares to pull out, three vehicles are detached to rush the wounded Blackburn back to base.

4:15 P.M. Fighting and confusion delay loading the prisoners and pulling out.

4:20 P.M. Black Hawk Super Six One, piloted by Chief Warrant Officer Cliff Wolcott, known to his friends as "Elvis," is hit by a rocket-propelled grenade and crashes five blocks northeast of the target building.

4:22 P.M. Crowds of Somalis race toward the crash site. The convoy and ground forces begin moving toward the downed chopper. Black Hawk Super Six Four, piloted by Chief Warrant Officer Mike Durant, takes the crashed helicopter's place in orbit over the fight.

4:28 P.M. A search-and-rescue team ropes in to assist the downed crew.

4:35 P.M. The U.S. convoy makes a wrong turn and becomes lost in the labyrinthine city streets of Mogadishu, encountering roadblocks at every turn and sustaining heavy casualties.

4:40 P.M. Durant's Black Hawk, Super Six Four, is also hit and crashes about a mile southwest of the target building. Hostile crowds begin moving toward the downed chopper.

4:42 P.M. Two Delta Force snipers, Sgts. Randy Shughart and Gary Gordon, volunteer to be inserted at the second crash site by helicopter to help protect the injured Durant and his crew.

4:54 P.M. The "Lost Convoy," with more than half of its force wounded or dead, abandons its search for the first downed Black Hawk and begins fighting its way back to the American base on the Indian Ocean.

5:03 P.M. A smaller, emergency convoy is dispatched in an attempt to rescue the men stranded at Durant's crash site. It encounters fires, roadblocks, and other obstacles.

5:34 P.M. Both convoys, battered and bleeding, link up and abandon the effort to break through to Durant at the second crash site. The remaining ground force of Rangers and Delta commandos converge around the first crash site, sustaining many casualties.

5:40 P.M. Somali crowds overrun Durant's crash site, killing Shughart and Gordon and the rest of the crew, except the wounded Durant, who is taken hostage and carried off by Somali militia.

5:45 P.M. Both convoys return to the base. Ninety-nine men remain trapped and surrounded in the city around the first downed Black Hawk, fighting for their lives.

10:00 P.M. A giant convoy—with two companies of the 10th Mountain Division along with the remainder of Task Force Ranger, as well as Pakistani tanks and Malaysian armored vehicles under the U.N. peacekeeping force—begins to form to rescue the trapped soldiers.

11:23 P.M. The huge rescue convoy moves out, blazing into Mogadishu.

October 4, 1993

1:55 A.M. The rescue convoy reaches the trapped Ranger force. The night belongs to the U.S. "Nightstalkers"—crack pilots of the 160th SOAR—as they make innumerable strafing runs with heavily-armed Little Bird attack helicopters to protect their comrades in the streets below.

3:00 A.M. Forces struggle to remove the pinned body of Wolcott, pilot of Super Six One, determined to follow the creed of leaving no man behind, living or dead.

| 5:30 A.M. | Wolcott's body is finally recovered, and the rescue convoy begins to roll out of the city. But with the vehicles packed with 10th Mountain and U.N. forces, the Rangers are left to run "The Mogadishu Mile" through considerable gunfire behind the convoy. |
| 6:30 A.M. | The force returns to the safety of a U.N.-controlled sports stadium with 18 dead and 73 injured. The casualties among the Somalis has never been confirmed, but is thought to be approximately 500 dead and many more wounded. |

March 8, 2001: A New Mission

The first day of filming in Kenitra, Morocco, on *Black Hawk Down*. From the time he read Mark Bowden's book in galley form, producer Jerry Bruckheimer knew that it was time for a new mission: to bring it to the screen as vividly and authentically as possible. "I read the book before it came out in bookstores, and fell in love with it," states Bruckheimer.

Bowden, a journalist of repute for *The Philadelphia Inquirer*, began working on the story some two-and-a-half years after the battle was fought, when it had already begun to fade from the news—perceived by the media as a military fiasco and early foreign affairs failure of President Bill Clinton's administration. Bowden became intrigued by the details of the battle itself and its aftermath. Who were these men who fought on that long day's journey into night? What were their feelings?

After some initial research, the battle was humanized for Bowden when he was invited by Jim Smith—the father of Cpl. Jamie Smith, a Ranger who was tragically killed in the battle—to a dedication ceremony of a building being named in the young man's honor. There he met about 12 Rangers who had fought in Mogadishu with Jamie, and all agreed to be interviewed. This was the beginning of a path which led Bowden to years of additional research, a multitude of interviews, and an actual, perilous journey into Somalia in the summer of 1997. The book that emerged, entitled *Black Hawk Down: A Story of Modern War*, was published in 1999 to great acclaim for its detail and evenhandedness.

"No matter how critically history records the policy decisions that led up to this fight," wrote Bowden in his conclusion, "nothing can diminish the professionalism and dedication of the Rangers and Special Forces units who fought there that day." It was this approach to the matter that so intrigued Bruckheimer.

Ridley Scott: A Story to Tell

To bring Bowden's book to the screen, Bruckheimer called upon Ridley Scott, one of the film industry's acknowledged visionaries. Bruckheimer already had a longtime association with Ridley's brother Tony Scott, who had directed five of the producer's megahits. However, he hadn't yet had the opportunity to collaborate on a feature with Ridley Scott, whom Bruckheimer deems "one of the greatest directors living today. He's a world-renowned artist as a filmmaker. Ridley's movies have lives of their own."

Ridley Scott remembers full well his response to the actual incidents reported in Bowden's book. "I was in London at the time, and I recall watching BBC News and seeing this tragic sight of what was clearly two bodies that were being seriously mauled. And I realized, my God, those are U.S. troops. I'd already spent 20 odd years in and out of the United States, and I pretty well had a handle on how Americans respond to such things. I knew that it would be a giant shock to the system, seeing that being pushed into the forefront of their lives on the television sets at home."

After reading Mark Bowden's book, Scott was immediately taken with the idea of filming it. He had already re-created ancient warfare in *Gladiator*, and with *Black Hawk Down* saw the opportunity to tell a timeless and timely story of men in combat. Although there have been war films by the thousands, very few have set out to portray in detail just one battle rather than sweeping conflicts. For *Black Hawk Down*, Scott sought to create an unflinching, uncompromising portrait of war, with all of its attendant horrors, heartbreak, and, at times, undeniable heroism.

As in the book, Scott was determined to create a story of combat that eliminated any information except what was occurring during the battle. It was not in his interest to create "back stories" for each of the soldiers, or for the audience to learn their histories before or after the battle. Anything revealed of their personal world emerged in their actions during the mission.

Book into Screenplay

A great challenge facing Bruckheimer and Scott was how to translate the complexities of Bowden's book into a viable feature film. "The event itself took about 16 hours from the start of the mission until it ended, and of course we can't spend 16 hours in a theater," notes Bruckheimer.

"The book is like a giant jigsaw puzzle of cause and effect," adds Scott. "As the pieces start to come together, it forms into the very anatomy of a war which takes place in 16 hours. I thought it was a fairly formidable task to put it in screenplay form."

Helping Bruckheimer and Scott fashion the book into a workable screenplay was young writer Ken Nolan, who through 10 years of scribing in Hollywood had sold some scripts but never seen his work come to fruition on screen. "It was an amazing read," says Nolan of Bowden's book. "What struck me about *Black Hawk Down* was that it was a war book that put the reader right in the soldiers' boots."

"The book follows the fortunes of almost 100 soldiers," notes Bruckheimer, "and of course, that would have been impossible on film. I think what's remarkable about the screenplay is that we still get to know 40 characters, and live the battle through their experiences."

"The thing is, all these guys were heroes," adds executive producer Mike Stenson. "The reason they ended up in a 16-hour firefight was that they went to rescue their fallen comrades instead of going back to base and waiting for reinforcements. We wanted to make sure we paid tribute to the group while focusing on certain characters for dramatic purposes." (In the film, the characters of Sgt. First Class "Hoot" Gibson, Spec. Grimes, Sgt. First Class Jeff Sanderson, and Master Sgt. Chris "Wex" Wexler are fictionalized composites of real soldiers; however, the rest of those depicted bear the actual names of their real-life counterparts).

The filmmakers decided that "The story will be seen through a number of eyes in a large ensemble," adds Bruckheimer, "but to a great extent through a young Ranger sergeant, Matt Eversmann, who takes over the command of Chalk Four after its leader, Beales, has an epileptic seizure the night before the mission.

"Eversmann's counterpart," explains Bruckheimer, "is a toughened Delta Force operator known as 'Hoot,' who is the ultimate soldier in one of the most elite units. 'Hoot' has 'been there and done that,' and acts as a kind of mysterious older brother figure to Eversmann, who is inexperienced in actual combat."

"Audiences have to care about these men," adds Ken Nolan. "At the end of the day, I'm hoping that people will really make an emotional investment in these people and incidents."

Calling in the Experts

As the screenplay came together, so did the rest of the primary production team. Coming into the *Black Hawk Down* fold in crucial positions were longtime collaborators of Ridley Scott's—most of whom had worked on *Gladiator* or *Hannibal*, or both. Many of Jerry Bruckheimer's associates also enlisted—most prominently Key Military/Technical Advisor Harry Humphries, who had worked with the producer on several projects from *The Rock* to *Enemy of the State* and *Pearl Harbor*. Humphries has also collaborated with Ridley Scott on *G.I. Jane.*

"Jerry's the ideal person and friend for me to work with," notes Humphries, "because he's always looking for accuracy—as much as film will allow—and he's not going to compromise. He will always vote in favor of accuracy with respect to military or law enforcement activities, as opposed to the Hollywood view of how it should look."

Chosen by Bruckheimer and Scott as director of photography was Slawomir Idziak of Poland, who had impressed them with his remarkably sensitive, even experimental, work on several of the late Krzysztof Kieslowski's films and who had also demonstrated an ability to handle such bigger-budgeted action films as *Proof of Life.* Bruckheimer and Scott were impressed by Idziak's visual dexterity and experimental use of color washes to underscore atmosphere and psychology.

As he had on *Schindler's List, Gladiator,* and *Hannibal,* executive producer Branko Lustig—with some 50 years of moviemaking experience around the world—would handle the tremendous day-to-day responsibilities of keeping the production on track. "I am only here to help the filmmakers make the movie," notes Lustig, "and I knew as soon as I read the script that the production would be very difficult because of all the smaller stories being told within the larger framework. Here we have nonstop action, often with incidents happening parallel to each other. And although Ridley is a master at controlling the set, I knew that shooting would be enormously complex."

Finding East Africa in North Africa

Fifty years ago, if a filmmaker wanted to shoot against an exotic backdrop, it was usually built on a backlot in Hollywood. Nowadays, Hollywood goes out into the world and films Paris in Paris, Tokyo in Tokyo, or Kathmandu in Kathmandu.

However, the notion of actually filming *Black Hawk Down* in Somalia could never be more than a fantasy, for the onetime vacation destination for wealthy Italians is, unfortunately, as anarchic and dangerous now as it was in 1993. "When I first read the book," recalls Branko Lustig, "I told Ridley that I would go to Mogadishu to scout but soon discovered that no one issues visas for

Somalia. The only way to get to Mogadishu is to travel to Ethiopia and then try and hire a boat to take you there. It's not exactly practical."

"Mogadishu is a no-go zone," adds production designer Arthur Max. "It's dangerous and overrun by armed militias. So knowing that it would be impossible to film there, we decided to scout locations in the Mediterranean area, including Israel, Jordan, Egypt, as well as southern Spain and all of North Africa. We finally settled on the area of Rabat and its neighboring city of Sale, on the Atlantic coast of Morocco, as they were the closest in all the research materials we had seen—photographs and films—to the architecture and terrain of Mogadishu."

"We had to do this film relatively quickly," says Ridley Scott, "because we started in March and were going to release in December of the same year. It's really about decisions, and how fast you make them. While I was mixing *Hannibal*, I asked Branko and Arthur to scout locations. We looked at the photographs they came back with and went straight into Morocco. That's how you get a kick start."

Branko Lustig had already done other films partially in Morocco and had wide knowledge of that country's film industry and its personnel. Over the years, he had gotten to know and befriend the noted Moroccan film director Souheil Ben Barka, who had since become head of the Moroccan film commission known as the CCM (Centre Cinematographique Marocaine). "I had some guarantees from Mr. Ben Barka and the governor of Sale that we could film there, and after Jerry and Ridley approved the locations I returned to Morocco with a letter for His Majesty King Mohammed VI, sending him a script that had been translated into French.

"The king and his ministers reacted positively," continues Lustig, "feeling that it was about an historical event and was in no way slanted against Muslims. They not only agreed to allow us to film there, but also put a great deal of Moroccan military materiel, from tanks to Humvees and helicopters, at our disposal."

It was to be a propitious choice. Rabat, the capital, is a progressive, French and Arabic-speaking North African city with a good infrastructure, which could provide the necessary hotel accommodations, restaurants, and attractions for a huge cast and crew looking at more than four months of location filming. The ancient city of Sale, across the Bou Regreg River from Rabat, featured remarkable similarities to Mogadishu. Both are cities at the edge of a great ocean (albeit on opposite sides of the African continent), but unlike Somalia, Morocco could afford the filmmakers the cooperation of King Mohammed

VI, the authorities at the CCM, and their expert, highly experienced film workers.

"Morocco is also such a beautiful and culturally rich country," Bruckheimer adds, "so there's a lot for the cast and crew to do on off days. They could travel to Marrakesh, Fez, Casablanca or Tangier, or even to southern Spain, which is just a few hours away from Rabat. Even in the city, one can go to the ancient medina or get to know the Moroccan people, who are wonderful."

Casting An International Net

As Scott, Bruckheimer, and Lustig began organizing the giant production effort, the filmmakers also began to search for appropriate actors to inhabit the more than 40 principal roles in Nolan's screenplay. Despite the fact that the film focuses on American soldiers, Scott felt in no way inhibited by the separation of cultures or continents, for in the end he cast not only a large group of Americans, but also selected talented actors from the British continent (English, Scottish and Welsh) and even one from Denmark.

"I just look for good actors," Scott states, "wherever they happen to be from. It was tricky to cast this ensemble, because there are some 40 speaking roles. All of them are important, and it's always sensitive when you're talking to an actor who's accustomed to a bigger role, and they're saying 'Well, I've only got four scenes.' I say, 'Yeah, but they're four really *good* scenes.' So it was a hard process of casting and persuading them what a good project it was going to be, and that all the effort would be worth it." In fact, most actors in *Black Hawk Down* were more than willing to cast their egos aside for the opportunity of working with Ridley Scott and Jerry Bruckheimer on a project of such significance.

Of key importance, of course, was casting the key roles of Eversmann and "Hoot." Bruckheimer and Scott were in full agreement as to who they wanted as the lead—Josh Hartnett, one of America's most talented young actors who had just starred for the producer with Ben Affleck and Kate Beckinsale in *Pearl Harbor*. Says Bruckheimer, "I think Josh is unique in that while he has undeniably 'heartthrob' appeal, he's a young actor of genuine commitment and depth who completely immerses himself in his work. There's a remarkable vulnerability and humanity about him, which was perfect for the role of Matt Eversmann."

Eric Bana, cast as the enigmatic Delta Sgt. First Class "Hoot" Gibson, came to Bruckheimer and Scott's attention from his native Australia, where he had carved out a big reputation, first as a stand-up comic and star of his own TV series, and then for his astonishing starring role as complex sociopath Mark "Chopper" Read in the feature film *Chopper*.

Another fine talent from across the ocean to make the leap was Ewan McGregor, the young Scot whose remarkable escalating range of roles from *Trainspotting* to portraying Obi Wan Kenobi in *Star Wars Episode 1: The Phantom Menace* and his musical wooing of Nicole Kidman in *Moulin Rouge* had made him one of the most sought-after talents in film. Two other principal actors were already well known to Jerry Bruckheimer, for both had performed in his other films: Tom Sizemore and William Fichtner, respectively portraying Ranger Lt. Col. Danny McKnight and Delta Sgt. First Class Jeff Sanderson.

To portray Major General William F. Garrison, a man still standing in the judgment of history for his command of the mission, Bruckheimer and Scott turned to an American icon—Sam Shepard, the Pulitzer Prize-winning playwright who had also become one of the country's most versatile and respected actors. British actor Jason Isaacs, who had fought the Americans as a brutish British officer in the Revolutionary War epic *The Patriot*, was now to wear a more contemporary U.S. uniform as Ranger Captain Mike Steele.

To fill out the huge speaking cast, the filmmakers cast their nets in the extraordinary talent pool of the United States, Britain, and Europe, many of them leading players in their own right who were anxious to contribute to Bruckheimer and Scott's ensemble. As a support for the non-American actors, dialect coach Sandra Butterworth would be on set nearly every day, making certain that the *R*s weren't rolled and the *A*s were properly flattened.

The Army Signs On

Harry Humphries, a former Navy S.E.A.L. decorated for action in Vietnam and more recently a security and tactical training expert with his own company, has served as a key military or technical adviser on several Jerry Bruckheimer films. Once again, Bruckheimer called upon Humphries, not only as an on-set adviser but also to prepare the cast for their respective roles as U. S. Rangers, Delta Force operatives, and helicopter pilots.

Bruckheimer, Scott, and executive producers Mike Stenson, Chad Oman, and Branko Lustig laid the groundwork for what would become a remarkable association with the U.S. Department of Defense, which would provide extraordinary cooperation with the filmmakers, allowing them to tell their story authentically. While Bruckheimer had already established a strong relationship with the U.S. military and D.O.D. from *Top Gun* to *Pearl*

Harbor and other projects in between, *Black Hawk Down* is based on a mission that is still highly sensitive, even controversial.

However, as Bruckheimer notes, "Mark Bowden's book is on their reading list.... It was something the military embraced, wanting their officers and men to read it. The head of the Joint Chiefs of Staff, General Sheldon, is an admirer of the book, so when we went to Washington to meet with [former] Secretary of Defense William Cohen, they were very enthusiastic about the project."

The first and very tangible sign of such cooperation was the D.O.D.'s invitation to the actors to participate in orientation and training at the actual military bases of the branches they were portraying: Fort Benning, Georgia, for the Rangers; Fort Bragg, North Carolina, for Special Forces (including the Delta Force, so secretive that the Army still doesn't officially acknowledge its existence); and Fort Campbell, Kentucky, for the 160th SOAR (Special Operations Aviation Regiment) pilots.

"We felt that it was really important for the actors to actually become part of the military, even for a short time," Jerry Bruckheimer asserts. "And so, as we did with *Pearl Harbor*, we sent them for training—not a Hollywood boot camp, but practical orientation. There's nothing like reality. You can't fake it. We wanted the actors to have respect for the military and understand the physical challenges they go through. If you talk to any soldier who has been through a battle, they'll tell you that the only thing that saved their lives was either the man next to them or their training."

"Sending actors to 'boot camp' is almost a conventional thing to do now," says Ridley Scott, "but when you think about it, it makes all the sense in the world, because if any actor has any notions of being better than the next guy, that goes right out the window. If they weren't fit already, they're a hell of a lot fitter than they will ever be in their lives. And if they *were* fit already, then they're even fitter than they could possibly be!"

Adds Harry Humphries, "I'm a big believer in making sure that before we start filming a movie such as this one, that actors are taught the necessary weaponry and physical skills up front so that we don't have to coach them so intensely on the set during production. It serves no purpose, to my mind, to simply put them through a harassing 'boot camp' session up front so that they can simply say, 'Man, I've been through hell.' My response would be, 'Well, that's very impressive, but what *skills* have you learned?' So my concept is not to harass, but to train the actors in actual skills.

"This effort, involving three separate training commands, was unparalleled to any D.O.D. training program that has ever been put forth—a wonderful, cooperative effort."

Orientation ... Learning the Ropes

At Fort Benning, Ranger instructors felt a strong personal stake in *Black Hawk Down*. Many of them had fought there, many knew men who had died there. Ranger Training Detachment commandant First Sgt. James Hardy's goal was to ensure that the 21 actors had a good understanding of the Ranger mentality and way of life, and how events played out in Mogadishu over those two days.

Ranger instructors taught classes from general military knowledge (how to wear the uniform properly, customs, and courtesies) to advanced marksmanship skills. The actors learned the Ranger Creed and Ranger history, hand-to-hand combat techniques, how to tie knots and use radios. Hugh Dancy, who would portray medic Kurt "Doc" Schmid, worked with Ranger medics in combat scenarios. On the fourth day of training, the actors fired M16-A2 rifles and squad automatic weapons. While at Fort Benning, the actors got their "high-and-tight" Ranger haircuts, and wore desert-camouflage uniforms and nametags of their Ranger characters.

Remarked Ranger instructor Sgt. First Class Martin Barreras, "I want them to remember the sense of teamwork that is inherent to a Ranger organization and the amount of attention to detail that's required from every individual that is part of that team."

Josh Hartnett, who had already been through a training program for *Pearl Harbor*, faced a different set of goals for his portrayal of Sgt. Matt Eversmann, who had faced down the enemy in Mogadishu just eight years before. "We were taught how to move and think like a Ranger," notes the young actor. "They teach you slogans like 'Slow is smooth and smooth is fast,' which means that if you're bouncing around, you can't really see what's happening around you."

At Fort Bragg's Special Forces orientation, Eric Bana, William Fichtner, and Nikolaj Coster-Waldau received detailed instruction on the proper handling and operation of weapons used by the Delta Force soldiers in Somalia, as well as "breaching training" (entering locked or obstructed doorways or windows using explosives, and learning how to enter and clear a building of possible threats). On their final day, Bana, Fichtner, and Coster-Waldau trained at Fort Bragg's Urban Terrain site, a cinderblock mock village where Special Forces soldiers demonstrated movement through a city that poses threats at every turn...which Mogadishu certainly did on that fateful day and night in 1993.

Meeting actual Delta operators "helped in ways I couldn't have imagined," Eric Bana says, "and not only in terms of learning tactics and weaponry. Since there were only three of us, we spent a lot of time with our instructors. We'd go out to dinner with them, hang out, and really get to know them. They were very worldly, extremely well-read, incredibly intelligent, and had an amazing sense of humor. It gave me the confidence to go with things for my character that I had been thinking about, but wasn't quite sure were relevant. And it also allowed for an on-screen rapport between Bill, Nikolaj, and myself that was completely nonmanufactured."

Farther west, at Fort Campbell in Kentucky, Ron Eldard, and Jeremy Piven were learning some of the ropes of what it takes to be the best of the best with the men of the 160th SOAR, the legendary "Nightstalkers" (so called because of their expertise at night flying). The actors met with several veterans of Somalia, "flew" missions in the unit's flight simulator under the same conditions faced by Wolcott and Durant during the mission, and got an in-depth briefing by the recently retired Mike Durant himself.

Says Jeremy Piven, who portrays Chief Warrant Officer Cliff Wolcott, "Flying Black Hawks is incredibly intense. All of one's motor skills are needed at every moment, the controls are so responsive and delicate. We trained in simulators and studied the actual Black Hawks on the ground, and these machines are incredible, the highest level out there. They can maneuver into anything. They can fly at night. They're jet black, ominous. You have to be at the top of your game to fly them.

"Every pilot who came up to me during training said, 'Just do Cliff Wolcott proud, because he was the real deal. All we ask is that you all try to keep it real.'"

Keeping It Real ... The Filming of *Black Hawk Down*

Following their training, the international contingent of performers descended upon Rabat, Morocco, with a tremendous group of behind-the-scenes artists, craftsmen, and technicians from around the world organized by Jerry Bruckheimer, Ridley Scott, and Branko Lustig.

The crew of *Black Hawk Down* represented a truly awesome international coalition. The largest contingent was actually from home turf in Morocco, with expert workers hailing from every corner of the country. The second largest group was from Great Britain, including most of the special effects, props, wardrobe, set decorating, and armory departments. The better part of Arthur Max's art department hailed from Italy, artisans who had previously worked with him on the massive sets of *Gladiator*. Approximately 50 Americans, sprinkled through the production and other departments, traveled from New York, Los Angeles, and points in between. Branko Lustig, a native of Croatia, brought in some 50 of his former countrymen (and women) to work in various departments (again, many of whom were veterans of *Gladiator*), and the better part of the stunt players under coordinator Phil Neilson were from the Czech Republic, many of whom had also seen action in *Gladiator*'s bloodied ancient arenas.

Other countries represented on the crew were Canada, France, the West Indies, Germany, Ireland, Malta, Poland, Wales, Scotland, Ireland, Spain, Russia, Slovakia, Austria, New Zealand, Senegal, and even Thailand. All told, there were nearly a thousand crew members on the most demanding days, in addition to the huge cast and extras.

Further internationalizing the production was the dedicated group of extras assembled by William F. Dowd to portray the Somalis. "Since there are few, if any, Somalis living in Morocco," Dowd explains, "we had to organize people from some 30 other countries in Africa who are working or studying in and around Rabat. We attracted people from Nigeria, Burkina Faso, Ghana, Sierra Leone, Angola, Djibouti, Senegal, and Congo." Dowd also enlisted Moroccans and Berbers from the southern deserts, of sub-Saharan African descent. The Africans would create their own rich babel of languages, including Creole, Wolof, Dutch, Italian, French, English, and several tribal dialects. And with the aid of stunt coordinator Phil Neilson, 50 Africans were chosen as the core Somali militiamen. Intense physical and weapons training converted them into extraordinary stunt players.

Three British actors—Razaaq Adoti, Treva Etienne, and George Harris— were cast by Ridley Scott as major Somali characters. Adoti plays the fierce militiaman Mo'alim, Etienne is Black Hawk pilot Mike Durant's captor Firimbi, and polished, educated businessman Osman Atto is played by Harris. All were determined to bring a sense of humanity and balance to an "enemy" that had a firm belief in the righteousness of their cause.

Notes Adoti, "As an actor, if you're going to play someone who's responsible for despicable acts—even if it's alien and incomprehensible to yourself—you still have to find the truth and the reasons behind them so you can play the character believably. On a moral scale, Mo'alim is doing a lot of wrong. He's killing his own people. At the same time, I try to under-

166

stand that Somalia had been occupied by many nations, and this created a mistrust or even hatred of foreign armies in their midst. So Mo'alim sees the U.N. forces as just another occupying entity. As far as he's concerned, he's a Somali patriot doing the right thing for his people."

Production Design to the "Max"

Before actors and crew could begin filming, the physical backdrop needed to be created, and Ridley Scott turned to production designer Arthur Max. "At the beginning of the process," Max explains, "Ridley and I do a pinup of imagery on the walls, as much reference material as we can find. We whittle that down to things that resonate with us. Then we scout together on the ground and try to fit those images into the context of a situation."

"For *Black Hawk Down*," continues Max, "we worked with very large-scale models, as well as aerial photographs mapping sections of the city that we were interested in. We then developed the actual set designs and began to build them four months before shooting was scheduled to begin."

In effect, an entire neighborhood had to be "made over" from Morocco to Mogadishu. The area of Sale chosen as the primary backdrop for filming was a teeming, decidedly downscale, pungent working-class district called Sidi Moussa, composed of two- or three-story, mostly illegally constructed dwellings, and populated largely by rural Moroccans seeking a better life in the city. What Ridley Scott required for his cinematic vision was an African urban area large enough to be photographed from the ground and air—mostly without the benefit of visual effects—and resemble the grungy Somali capital of Mogadishu as closely as possible.

Comments Arthur Max, "In Sidi Moussa there's a rich array of walled cities from Crusader times, old medinas, half-completed new towns, coastal roads, cemeteries, areas of abandonment, and some very fine architecture, with beautiful markets and mosques. In effect, it was a tremendous back lot set for us."

Major set construction took place in several parts of Sidi Moussa, with crews of at least 150 in each location working simultaneously. Several sets were built from scratch, others were added on to existing buildings or basically used as found. Several blocks of Avenue Nasser were convincingly re-created as downtown Mogadishu. Facades of residential buildings were completely refaced to eliminate recognizable Moroccan design motifs, and pockmarked with bullet and shell holes. Street after street of tumbledown buildings was strewn with copious amounts of rubbish, burnt-out vehicles, roadblocks, and other detritus of war. In all, some 35 square blocks of "downtown Sidi Moussa" were transformed into the war-torn backdrop of Mogadishu.

Notes Max, "We tried to re-create the ambiance of Mogadishu with its very layered history of generations of occupancy by various powers. The Ottoman Turks, Italians, and British were there, and finally a Soviet-backed puppet government."

To serve as the U.S. military base in Mogadishu, Jerry Bruckheimer and Branko Lustig arranged with the Moroccan government to use a working Royal Moroccan Air Force field some 20 miles north of Rabat in the coastal town of Kenitra, creating sets inside of hangars and building other structures. Even for this utilitarian set, Scott and Max's visual creativity resulted in a fascinatingly designed makeshift barracks for the Rangers and Delta Force soldiers, where set decorator Elli Griff and her team extraordinarily detailed each man's diminutive personal space with personal effects true to his character and the early 1990s setting.

The only set not built in a "practical" location was the JOC, or Joint Operations Center, the headquarters from which Maj. General Garrison commands the mission, tracking the fate of his men on banks of television monitors. But even the JOC was constructed in Sale's "Zone Industrielle," inside an abandoned warehouse. Yet another huge, half-developed chunk of Sidi Moussa was utilized for the climactic "Mogadishu Mile," in which the desperate, exhausted Rangers run through withering enemy fire to the safety of a U.N.-held sports stadium in the north of the city.

Epic Story, Epic Filming

To be on the set of *Black Hawk Down* in Sale during filming was to witness a daily spectacle that sometimes defied description. Thousands of actors and extras arrayed in uniform or Somali native costume, myriad weaponry, fearsome explosions and fires, hovering helicopters either photographing the action or being photographed from both ground and air—all in the midst of a population either fascinated or puzzled by the incredible activities of the cast and crew. Tremendous base camps were set up for both first and second units, with a huge array of campers, trailers, trucks, and other production vehicles, and tents. Dozens of military vehicles— Humvees, tanks, trucks, and Somali "technicals" (dilapidated pickup trucks with jerry-mounted .50 caliber machine guns)—were also housed at the base camps when not in use on the set.

While the inhabitants of Sidi Moussa and other districts of Sale were occasionally inconvenienced or unnerved by filming, the production also provided an extraordinary number of jobs or financial compensation, welcome in a district with 85 percent unemployment. Most of the residents of Sale displayed remarkable cooperation and friendliness toward the cinematic visitors, often inviting crew members inside their homes for the ubiquitous Moroccan mint tea and sweets.

"When we first got to Sidi Moussa," recalls Ridley Scott, "some of us said, 'Wow, it's pretty rough here.' But when you got used to going there every day, it was actually rather nice. We'd have practically the entire town there every day, just watching."

To properly film the expansive action setpieces, Scott and director of photography Slawomir Idziak would normally shoot with multiple camera setups, six to eight on average, with many more for the bigger sequences. Unlike many action films, in which scenes are shot in 30- to 45-second segments, Scott preferred filming long, complex combat sequences from beginning to end, with cameras capturing specific moments as per their placement. This technique added to the spontaneity and authenticity of the battle scenes, and for spectators was rather like watching a real war.

Helping to run the show was first assistant director/associate producer Terry Needham, acknowledged as one of the best, most experienced and most unyielding in his profession. A colorful veteran of several films with Ridley Scott and the late Stanley Kubrick, Needham and his production crew somehow managed to hold the diverse elements together.

"It looked like chaos," notes Branko Lustig, "but it was organized chaos. Everybody knew what he or she was doing. It was an enormous crew with everybody speaking different languages, but somehow, when Ridley called 'Action!,' everything functioned."

The weapons department was supervised by Simon Atherton, one of the foremost armorers in motion pictures. Atherton and his mostly English crew had to assemble a mighty arsenal, including Soviet-made AK-47 assault rifles, rocket-propelled grenades (RPGs), and "technical"-mounted recoilless rifles used by the Somalis; and for the Americans, M-16 automatic rifles, Browning .50 caliber machine guns (with their earsplitting reports), LAWs (Light Antitank Weapons), M-60 machine guns, SAWs (Squad Automatic Weapons), and lethal miniguns mounted on the helicopters—electric-powered machine guns capable of firing up to 4,000 rounds per minute. All were retrofitted to shoot blank cartridges, and were often duplicated in amazingly realistic, nonfiring rubber replicas for nonfiring extras.

Stunt coordinator Phil Neilson called upon his own background in the American military to create complex stunts and combat action. "Number one in our minds," says Neilson, "was the safety of cast, crew, extras, and the people living where we were filming" (by the end of filming, there wasn't a single major injury). It was also important to follow Ridley Scott's dictum to keep the action within the bounds of reality. "I'm not crazy about over-the-top Hollywood hokum," notes Neilson. "I like realism, and it was important to keep *Black Hawk Down* gritty and authentic."

Also crucial in helping to create battlefield mayhem was special effects supervisor and prosthetics supervisor Neil Corbould, an Academy Award® winner for his work on *Saving Private Ryan*, and his large crew of technicians. "I've done war movies before where a section of the movie is combat, but there are quieter moments in between," says Courbould. "But in this, it's nonstop bullet hits, explosions, and helicopters crashes. Almost every shot in the battle scenes lasts quite a long time, which requires full effects, so we had some 40 guys on the floor working flat-out."

Corbould and his crew would also construct several full- or nearly full-sized mockups of the Black Hawks, including the remains of the crashed Super Six One and Super Six Four. Most remarkable, perhaps, was the helicopter gimbal mounted on a high crane that Corbould designed and built for sequences with the key actors inside the Black Hawks as they fly or hover over Mogadishu. Scott, for the sake of authenticity, wanted no old-fashioned optical "blue screen" visual effects shots.

Because of the radio-controlled explosions and squib hits, cell phones—endemic on movie sets—were strictly banned from the filming area under penalty of dismissal, because they might accidentally set off the effects so carefully arranged by Corbould and his team.

The Advisers

Also helping to "keep it real" were Military Adviser Harry Humphries and two key members of his staff, both of whom had been deeply involved in the actual battle and had only recently retired from the military. Col. Thomas Matthews, air commander of the mission who circled above the battle in the "C-2 Bird," the Command and Control Black Hawk, was unit commander of the "Nightstalkers," the helicopter organization that supports the Special Operations ground forces worldwide. Special Forces Col. Lee Van Arsdale was the officer in charge of the Joint Operations Center, who helped lead the rescue convoy into Mogadishu to rescue the trapped Rangers and Delta Force troops.

"Harry Humphries plays such an important role on set," notes Jerry Bruckheimer, "working with the actors and extras day to day to make sure everything looks accurate. It was also invaluable having Tom and Lee with us, because they went through it and could answer any question that Ridley might have. They helped our effort tremendously."

"Going to Morocco was not exactly what I had planned to do with my retirement," admits Matthews, "but for the memory of the soldiers who were killed in that combat operation and their families, I came to the conclusion that I would put my second career on hold and do the best job I could to technically advise on the movie."

Van Arsdale also saw an opportunity to finally set the record straight. "A fact that I think has been lost on a lot of people—but certainly not those of us who participated in it—was that from a military and tactical perspective, we had a successful mission. We had a job to get two of Aidid's top lieutenants and any of their bodyguards who may have been around that day, and that's exactly what we did."

Also with a great personal stake in telling the story was utility stunt player John Collett, who as a Ranger Specialist was in one of the four chalks that fast-roped down to the target building in "the Mog," then proceeded to fight throughout the rest of the day and night alongside his buddies. Throughout production, Collett relived his experiences on a daily basis, which was not always easy.

"I believe we went to Mogadishu for the right reasons," affirms Collett. "I believe that certain things went wrong that day. I met a couple of Somalis working as extras on this film who were actually in Mogadishu on October 3, 1993. We sat down and talked, had a few beers together, and they actually showed me some photographs of one of the Black Hawks after it had been shot down. Now, that was an experience! Eight years later, to be sitting across the table in the bar of the Rabat Hilton with people who were on the ground. Whether or not they were shooting at me at the time, I'll never know. Were they? Probably. But they were good people, and believed in what they were doing as well."

The "Insertion"... History Comes to Life

Greatest of all the herculean tasks facing the commanders of *Black Hawk Down* was the extraordinarily sensitive negotiations between the production, the

Moroccan government, and the U.S. State Department and Department of Defense to allow approximately 100 U.S. Rangers, four Black Hawks, four Little Birds and their pilots from the 160th SOAR—and backup military personnel accompanying them—to fly across the Atlantic and help the production properly re-create the mission with utmost verisimilitude.

Even before recent events, the notion of bringing armed forces and materiel of the United States to a sovereign North African kingdom with a Muslim population—however friendly relations might be between the countries—was far-reaching, to say the least.

"However enthusiastic the U.S. government was about our project," says Jerry Bruckheimer, "there were still bureaucracies to deal with and many voices to be heard. There were issues to be worked out between the State Department and the Moroccan government, and it took a lot longer than we expected. Even though we have a great relationship with the government, this was a much bigger operation than anything we had attempted before, even on *Top Gun* and *Pearl Harbor*. We were talking about actual troop deployment."

Admits Ridley Scott, "There was a lot of negotiation and a lot of anxiety."

For several days after filming commenced, there were rumors of imminent "delivery" of the men and equipment, only to be dashed at the last minute. Notes Branko Lustig, "How do you make a movie called *Black Hawk Down* without Black Hawks? You cannot independently buy these helicopters for filmmaking purposes. They are the property of the United States Armed Forces. We had a last-minute plan that if we couldn't get the Black Hawks, we would use Huey helicopters, and then digitally alter them afterwards to look like Black Hawks ... but that was really the worst-case scenario."

The tremendously complex "insertion" scene, in which the mission begins at the target building in downtown Mogadishu, was postponed again and again. But finally, about 48 hours before the production would have had to elect to use Hueys, all the paperwork was signed and two C-5 transport planes landed at an airport near Rabat. Their cargo: more than 100 soldiers from the 3rd Batallion, Bravo Company of the 75th Ranger Regiment—the same company that fought in Mogadishu—and four Black Hawks and four Little Birds, along with their pilots.

Officially it was a training deployment, and nothing could have been more true, because Rangers and helicopters were to receive quite a workout on behalf of the movie. "The director told me what he needed for his cameras, and I had to come back to him with a military plan," explains

Major Brian Bean, Operations Officer from the 160th SOAR for the task force. "We've integrated very closely with the film's aerial coordinators. And on the artistic side, a member of our Task Force stood next to Ridley Scott, making sure we understood his vision and executed it to our standards and safety."

"What's unique about the military supporting this film," adds Lt. Col. Kirk Potts, the Task Force commander, "is that you actually had the units which participated in the military operation eight years ago here, doing it again. In fact, we have three or four of the actual veterans of that operation flying the helicopters while we film it."

On April 16, a multitude of cameras both on the ground and in the air began to roll. From his Aerospatiale "A-Star" helicopter, aerial director of photography John Marzano readied his gyro-stabilized Wescam camera system, with almost 360-degree reference. The faint sounds of helicopters in the distance became a mighty roar as the four Black Hawks and four Little Birds hit their marks above and near the target building. Ropes were thrown out of the hovering Black Hawks, and in the ferocious wind and dust kicked up by the chopper blades, U.S. Rangers brilliantly fast-roped 60 feet from air to ground, while the Little Birds deposited stuntmen portraying Delta troops on rooftops. Meanwhile, with precision timing, the 12-vehicle extraction convoy rumbled to the front of the target building from a nearby street, as hundreds of extras portraying Somalis either ran from the mayhem—or toward it—weapons in hand.

For the benefit of different angles, this sequence of surpassing complexity would be replayed again for the cameras no fewer than eight times over the following two days.

"It was an awesome sight to see," exclaims Jerry Bruckheimer. "This isn't a movie where we're using a lot of computer-generated imagery. It's the real deal, and I've never seen anything quite like it. They did an amazing job."

"We probably had the best flying team from the U.S. Armed Forces," enthuses Ridley Scott, "and these guys came in and treated filming like a serious exercise. They loved it, and repetition was no problem, but we had to abide by their rules. They had to be in the air and down again by such-and-such time. And they were only allowed to fly a certain number of hours per day, and if we asked for seven more minutes, the answer was quite simply, 'No.'"

Witnessing the re-creation of the insertion was *Black Hawk Down* author Mark Bowden, who commented, "You really can do things on film that you can't do in a book, and the visuals in this movie are going to be extraordinary. Just being here on set and watching them re-enact this raid...it's a very powerful image. When I wrote the book, I had to imagine the insertion in great detail, but the film will show people things they've never seen before."

Military and moviemakers began to form something of a mutual admiration society—cast and crew members in absolute awe of the commitment and precision of the Rangers and SOAR pilots, and vice versa. "Our guys have a newfound respect for the cameramen, grips, stunt people, and everyone else working on *Black Hawk Down*," noted Major Bill Butler of the 75th Ranger Regiment. "We didn't realize how much work actually goes into making a movie."

"I think we originally had some apprehension," admitted Major Bean. "We were very concerned with the legacy of our fallen comrades and wanted to make sure that it was the first thing in everybody's mind. But once we got on the ground, we really enjoyed the professionalism of the production company, and they've showed us that they totally care about the memory of our men."

Mission Accomplished

Principal photography of *Black Hawk Down* was completed on June 29, 2001, after 92 days of filming, right where it started: at the Royal Moroccan Air Force Base in Kenitra. Back in Sidi Moussa, the art department not only restored the buildings on Avenue Nasser to their pre-Mogadishu look, but gave them an attractive facelift. The Target Building was dismantled, and the empty field could once again be used for pick-up soccer games. For the inhabitants of Sale, life returned to normal, although many later claimed to miss the excitement of production.

After four exhausting and exhilarating months, the filmmakers finally had time to reflect upon their experiences breathing life into recent history...and what they hoped audiences would take away from the film after seeing it.

"At the end of the day, I think that *Black Hawk Down* is very much from the universal soldier's point of view," offers Ridley Scott. "The Somali militiamen, though less trained and equipped than the Americans, were nevertheless very efficient. Therefore, what happened in Mogadishu became the meeting of two groups of fervent soldiers. As 'Hoot' says in the movie, 'once that first bullet goes past your head, politics goes right out the window.' Then it becomes about looking after the man next to you and getting the job done.

"But in the end," says the director, "are the obvious questions about whether or not the United States had a right to be in Somalia. And I think that when there's a humanitarian issue on the baseline, the answer is...yes...yes...and yes. Somebody's got to go in and do it, and it really falls at the feet of the U.S. because of the country's weight, prestige, and power.

"In October 1993, we all watched the bodies of the dead American soldiers on television, said, 'Oh my God,' and turned the channel to something more cheerful. But the world was already changing eight years ago, and how much it's changed was, unfortunately, illuminated on September 11. And the lesson is that if you don't watch the back door, somebody will come through it..."

Appendix: "The Ranger Creed"

Recognizing that I volunteered as a Ranger, fully knowing the hazards of my chosen profession, I will always endeavor to uphold the prestige, honor, and high "esprit de corps" of the Rangers.

Acknowledging the fact that a Ranger is a more elite soldier who arrives at the cutting edge of battle by land, sea, or air, I accept the fact that as a Ranger my country expects me to move further, faster and fight harder than any other soldier.

Never shall I fail my comrades. I will always keep myself mentally alert, physically strong and morally straight and I will shoulder more than my share of the task whatever it may be. One hundred percent and then some.

Gallantly will I show the world that I am a specially selected and well trained soldier. My courtesy to superior officers, my neatness of dress and care of equipment shall set the example for others to follow.

Energetically will I meet the enemies of my country. I shall defeat them on the field of battle for I am better trained and will fight with all my might. Surrender is not a Ranger word. I will never leave a fallen comrade to fall into the hands of the enemy and under no circumstances will I ever embarrass my country.

Readily will I display the intestinal fortitude required to fight on to the Ranger objective and complete the mission, though I be the lone survivor.

RANGERS LEAD THE WAY!

CAST AND CREW CREDITS

REVOLUTION STUDIOS and JERRY BRUCKHEIMER FILMS Present
A JERRY BRUCKHEIMER Production In Association with SCOTT FREE Productions.

Directed by
Ridley Scott

Screenplay by
Ken Nolan

Based on the book by
Mark Bowden

Produced by
Jerry Bruckheimer
Ridley Scott

Executive Producers
Simon West
Mike Stenson
Chad Oman

Executive Producer
Branko Lustig

Director of Photography
Slawomir Idziak

Production Designer
Arthur Max

Editor
Pietro Scalia, A.C.E.

Music by
Hans Zimmer

Josh Hartnett

BLACK HAWK DOWN

Ewan McGregor

Tom Sizemore
Eric Bana

William Fichtner
Ewen Bremner
and Sam Shepard

Gabriel Casseus
Kim Coates
Hugh Dancy

Ron Eldard
Ioan Gruffudd
Thomas Guiry

Charlie Hofheimer
Danny Hoch
Jason Isaacs

Željko Ivanek

Glenn Morshower

Jeremy Piven

Brendan Sexton III

Johnny Strong

Richard Tyson

Brian Van Holt
Nikolaj Coster-Waldau
Steven Ford
Ian Virgo
Thomas Hardy
Gregory Sporleder
Carmine Giovinazzo
Chris Beetem
Tac Fitzgerald
Matthew Marsden
Orlando Bloom
Kent Linville
Enrique Murciano
Michael Roof
George Harris
Razaaq Adoti
Treva Etienne

Abdibashir Mohamed Hersi

Casting by
Bonnie Timmermann

Costume Designers
Sammy Howarth-Sheldon
David Murphy

Music Supervision by
Kathy Nelson
Bob Badami

Associate Producers
Terry Needham
Harry Humphries
Pat Sandston

Revolution Studios and
Jerry Bruckheimer Films Present

in association with Scott Free
A Film by Ridley Scott

For My Mum
Elizabeth Jean Scott
1906 – 2001

Unit Production Managers	Pamela Hochschartner
	Branko Lustig
First Assistant Director	Terry Needham
Key Second Assistant Director.	Darin John Rivetti
Second Unit Director	Alexander Witt
Second Unit First Assistant Director	Adam Somner
Special Effects Supervisor	Neil Corbould
Unit Manager	Antoine L. Douaihy
Production Supervisors.	Lucio Trentini
	Angela Quiles
Art Directors	Pier Luigi Basile
	Marco Trentini
	Gianni Giovagnoni
	Ivica Husnjak
	Keith Pain
	Cliff Robinson
Set Decorator	Elli Griff
Property Master	Graeme Purdy
Camera & Steadicam Operator	Daniele Massaccesi
Camera Operator.	Martin Kenzie
Gaffer.	Marek Modzelewski
Key Grip.	David Appleby
Aerial Director of Photography	John Marzano
Key Makeup	Fabrizio Sforza
Key Hair Stylist	Giancarlo DeLeonardis
Costumers	Neil Murphy
	Diane Murphy
Key Armorer	Simon Atherton
Script Supervisor	Sally Jones
Production Accountant	Donna Glasser
Production Mixer	Chris Munro
Supervising Sound Editors	Per Hallberg
	Karen M. Baker
Re-Recording Mixers	Michael Minkler
	Myron Nettinga
Associate Editor	Wes Sewell
Post Production Supervisor	Teresa Kelly
VFX Supervisor	Tim Burke
VFX Producer	Emma Norton
First Assistant Camera	Henryk Jedynak
	Marco Sacerdoti
Second Assistant Camera	Fionn Comerford
	Basil Smith
Camera Technician	Stefan Baur

Remote Head Technician	Hans Lehner
Boom Operator	Andrew Griffiths
Still Photographer.	Sidney Baldwin
Video Operator	Michal Bukojemski
Video Assist	Lester Dunton
24 Frame Video Supervisor	Paul Conti
24 Frame Video Effects	Joe Conti
24 Frame Video Engineer.	Mark I. Scott
Costume Coordinator	Darryl M. Athons
Armorers.	Steve Cummings
	Tommy Dunne
	Alan Hausmann
	Nick Komornicki
	John Nixon
	Branko Repalust
	Trevor Rochester
Makeup	Alessandra Sampaolo
	Ana Bulajic Crcek
	Gianni Graziano
	Antonio Maltempo
Hair Stylists	Barbara DeLeonardis
. . . .	Michele Vigliotta
Chief Lighting Technician	Marek Modzelewski
Assistant Chief Lighting Technician.	Jacek Kurowski
Second Grip	Phil Murray
Key Rigging Electric	Dean Brkic
Rigging Best Boy	Željko Vrscak
First Assistant Editors.	ChisakoYokoyama
	Michael Reynolds
Assistant Editors	Valerio Bonelli
	Steven Sacks
	Robert Drwila
	Andrew Haigh
Apprentice Editors	Rex Teese
	Billy Rich
	Karen Hurley
Post Production Coordinators	Tami R. Goldman
	Jim Conrads
Assistant Set Decorator	Lisa Chugg
Set Dresser.	Mark Allett
Buyers.	Michael King
	Marissa Miller
Leadman.	Eric Mullet
Art Department Coordinator.	Annick Biltresse
Set Designers	Roberta Federico
	Monica Sallustio
Assistant Property Master	Steve Payne
Webbing Master	Petr Richter

Graphic Artist. . . . . Jim Stanes	Location & Extras Casting. . . . . William F. Dowd
Supervising Model Maker . . . . Toby Shears	U.K. Casting . . . . Suzanne M. Smith, CDG
Model Maker . . . . Dominic Weisz	Dialect Coach. . . . . Sandra Butterworth
Storyboard Artist. . . . . Sylvain Despretz	Casting Associate . . . . Seth Yanklewitz
Greensman . . . . Roger Holden	Casting Assistants . . . . Meagan Lewis
	Jose Cabrera
Unit Publicist . . . . Michael Singer	
Product Placement . . . . David B. Leener	Aerial Coordinators . . . . Marc Wolff
2nd Second Assistant Directors . . . . Basil Grillo	David Paris
Emma Horton	Aerial Cameraman. . . . . Michael Kelem
Hannah Quinn	Aerial First Assistant Cameraman . . . . Charlie Woodburn
Assistant Script Supervisor . . . . Zoe Morgan	Wescam Technician . . . . Clyde Miller
	Aerial Safety Coordinator . . . . Stephen J. North
Base Camp Managers . . . . Jonathan Hook	Aerial Military Coordinator . . . . Diana Latham
Mark Somner	Helicopter Pilots . . . . Bobby Zajonc
Location Facilities Manager . . . . . . Gregoire Mouveau	Jerry Grayson
Los Angeles Production Coordinator Kimberley Ann Berdy	Olaf Shumacher
Assistant Production Coordinators . . . . Damian Anderson	Freddy Rosenkranz
Rafael Lima	Dennis Kenyon
Shipping Coordinator . . . . Milena Bono Parodi	Francisco Paco Garcia
Travel Coordinator . . . . Carla Ferroni	Jose Garretta
Location Accountant . . . . Merrilee Dale	
First Assistant Accountants . . . . Jennifer P. Luther	Consultant . . . . Mark Bowden
Robin Reitman	Military Advisor . . . . Harry Humphries
Payroll Accountant. . . . . Kirby Adams	Military Consultants. . . . .
Construction Accountant . . . . Anil Patade	Colonel Thomas Matthews, USA Retired
Assistant Accountants . . . . Sven Reinhard	Colonel Lee Van Arsdale, USA Retired
Ernest Laurel	DOD USASOC Technical Advisor . . . .
Nicole Luther	Major Tom McCollum, USA
	Morocco Military Liaison . . . . Dragan Josipovic Joss
Production for JBF . . . . KristieAnne Reed	Research . . . . Vanessa Bendetti
Wynn Petersen	
Operations for JBF . . . . Tracy Pakulniewicz	First Aid . . . . Nicky Gregory
Assistants to Mr. Bruckheimer . . . . Orna Banarie	Trainer . . . . Steve Rosen
Andrea Bruce	Catering & Craft Service . . . . Rafael Catering
Justin Sperandeo	
Ryan Posly	Transportation Captains . . . . Ravi Dube
John Campbell	David Pash
Assistants to Mr. Scott . . . . Beth Vitallo	David Robling
Milly Leigh	
Special Advisor to Mr. Scott. . . . . . . Neville Shulman	Additional Re-Recording Mixers . . . . . . Gary A. Rizzo
Assistant to Mr. Lustig . . . . Aminta Townshend	Rick Ash
Assistant to Mr. Oman. . . . . Mary Viola	Sound Design Editor. . . . . Jon Title, M.P.S.E.
Assistant to Mr. Stenson . . . . Ed Walton	Supervising ADR Editors . . . . Chris Jargo
Production Assistants . . . . Tarik Ait Ben Ali	Anna MacKenzie
Toby E. Cook	Supervising Foley Editor. . . . . . Craig S. Jaeger, M.P.S.E.
Pierre Ellul	Supervising Dialogue Editor . Christopher Hogan, M.P.S.E.
Marielle Magne	First Assistant Sound Editor. . . Tony R. Negrete, M.P.S.E.
Ian Quiles	Assistant Sound Editors . . . . Philip D. Morrill
Patrick Michael Roddam	Todd Egan
India Salve-Guide	David Kudell
Dana Suman	
Kim Whittaker	

Sound Effects Editors	Christopher Assells, M.P.S.E.
	Dino R. DiMuro, M.P.S.E.
	Dan Hegeman, M.P.S.E.
	Michael A. Reagan
	Gregory J. Hainer, M.P.S.E.
	Perry Robertson
	Peter Staubli
	Bruce Tanis, M.P.S.E.
Dialogue Editors	Mark L. Mangino, M.P.S.E.
	Lauren Stephens, M.P.S.E.
	Stephanie Flack
ADR Editors	Laura Graham
	Michelle Pazer
	Zack Davis
	James A. Williams
ADR Mixer.	Thomas J. O'Connell
Foley Editors	Michael Hertlein
	Solange S. Schwalbe, M.P.S.E.
Foley Artists.	Dan O'Connell
	John Cucci
	John Roesch
	Alyson Moore
Foley Mixers	James Ashwill
	Mary Jo Lang
Recordists.	Andrea Eliseyan
	Eddie Bydalek
	Eric Flickinger
Group ADR Coordinator	Burt Sharp

Music Editor.	Marc Streitenfeld
Assistant Music Editor.	Del Spiva
Orchestrations.	Bruce Fowler
Music Contractor	Sandy DeCrescent
Music Clearance	Monica Ciafardini
Score Mixed by	Alan Meyerson
Score Recorded by	Greg Townley
	Mal Luker
	Al Clay
Assistant Engineers	Gregg Silk
	Kevin Globerman
	Jason Wormer
	TJ Lindgren
Sampling Engineer	Bart Hendrickson

Ambient Music by	Mel Wesson
Featured Vocalist.	Baaba Maal

BHD Band

Martin Tillman	Heitor Pereira
Craig Eastman	Michael Brook
Jeff Rona	

BHD Musicians

Mike Fisher	Brian Kilgore
John Fitzgerald	Ali Tavallali
Walt Fowler	Clay Duncan
Jim Dooley	Sam Maloney
Ilan Eshkeri	Satnum Ramgotra

Additional Score Cues
Performed by the BHD Band

"Pinned Down"	"Veils"
by Michael Brook	by Craig Eastman
"Mogadishu Blues"	"Réve Arabesque"
by Heitor Pereira	by Martin Tillman
"Bakara"	"Ascent"
by Jeff Rona	by Mel Wesson
"Wings"	
by Hans Zimmer	
and Baaba Maal	

Music Editor.	Marc Streitenfeld
Assistant Music Editor.	Del Spiva
Orchestrations.	Bruce Fowler
Music Contractor	Sandy DeCrescent
Music Clearance	Monica Ciafardini
Score Mixed by	Alan Meyerson
Score Recorded by	Greg Townley
	Mal Luker
	Al Clay
Assistant Engineers	Gregg Silk
	Kevin Globerman
	Jason Wormer
	TJ Lindgren

Music Production Services Provided by. . . . .
Media Ventures, Santa Monica, CA

Assistants to Mr. Zimmer

Moanike'ala Nakamoto	Trevor Morris
Kaz Boyle	Melissa Muik
Robert Bennett	

2nd UNIT

Unit Manager.	Alex Corven Caronia
Camera Operators	Ron Hersey
Steadicam Operator.	Zoran Mikincic
Key Grip	Cyril Kuhmholtz
Production Sound Mixer.	Tomo Fogec
Boom Operator	Damir Valincic
Set Dresser.	Antonio Murer

Aerial Safety Coordinator . . . . Philip Pickford		
Script Supervisor . . . . Nada Pinter		
Third Assistant Director . . . . William Dodds		
First Aid . . . . Rosie Bedford-Stradling		
Action Vehicle Coordinator . . . . Waldron LaMora		
Assistant Action Vehicle Coordinator. . . . . Mike Booys		

MOROCCO UNIT

Production Manager . . . . Jamal Souissi
First Assistant Directors . . . . Hatimi Ahmed
Rachid Gaidi
Second Assistant Directors . . . . Ali Cherkaoui
Zine-Eddine Ibnou Jabal
Camera Loaders. . . . . Abdellatif Ansary
Imad Rechiche
Camera Assistant . . . . Khalil El Mcherqui
Best Boy Electric. . . . . M. Najib Benfares
Key Grip . . . . Rifki Abdelghani
Production Secretary . . . . Widad Taha
Assistant Accountant . . . . Ibtisame Semmar
Control of Morocco Labor . . . . Samir Bounit
Buyer. Amine Rharda
Production Translators . . . . Fatima Laaouina
Karim Elamri
Makeup . . . . Malika Boukergane
Hair Stylist . . . . Hayat Ouleddahhou
Morocco Military Advisors. . . . . . . Colonel El Jaouhari
Captain Nabil Ghiadi
Location Manager . . . . Khalid Nekmouche
Morocco Casting Assistants . . . . Salah Benchegra
Gora Mbaye
Crowd Marshalls . . . . Mohamed Essaghir Aabach
Omar Tisli
Assistant to Mr. Souissi . . . . Houssna Choukri
Set Medic . . . . Dr. Celine Dechanet Painchaux
Catering & Craft Service. . . . . . . Societe Manzeh Diafa
Construction Buyer . . . . Said Arif Ahmed
Transportation Office Manager. . . . . Said Andam

Special Effects Wireman/Rigger . . . . . Stephen Crawley
Special Effects Senior Technicians . . . . . Barry Whitrod
Shaun Rutter
Alan Young
Ian Biggs
Special Effects Lead Technicians . . . . . . Steven Warner
David Watkins
Special Effects Technicians . . . . Joseph Geday
Gareth Wingrove
Anne Marie Walters
Simon Quinn
Mark Howard
Morocco Special Effects Coordinator . . . . Carol McAulay
Special Effects Supervising Plasterer . . . . David Baynham

Special Effects Unit Crew . . . . Abdelaali Berhich
Jamal Chrourou
Lahcen Harouane
Assistant Special Effects Supervisor . . Paul Grant Corbould
Special Effects Floor Supervisor. . . . . . Andrew Williams
Special Effects Workshop Supervisor . . . . David Brighton
Special Effects Lead Senior Technicians . Ian John Corbould
Clive Beard
Ian Wingrove
Prosthetics Effects Supervisor . . . . Neil Corbould
Prosthetics Assistant Supervisor . . . . . . John Schoonraad
Prosthetics Workshop Supervisors . . . . Cliff Wallace
David Hunter
Prosthetics Makeup Artists . . . . Simon Rose
Rob Mayor
Prosthetics Head Sculptor . . . . Roland Stevenson
Prosthetics Senior Technicians . . . . . Darren Robinson
Tristan Schoonraad
Michael Dunleavy

Visual FX by
MILL FILM

Executive Producer . . . . Robin Shenfield
Digital Supervisor . . . . Simon Stanley-Clamp
CG Supervisor . . . . Laurent Hugueniot
Production Supervisor. . . . . Susi Roper
VFX Coordinator . . . . Laya Armian
VFX Editor. . . . . Lars Vinther
Digital Color Timer . . . . Colin Coull
FX Elements by. . . . . Mill Models
Motion Control by . . . . Mill Motion Control

3D Artists

Alex Rothwell	Andy Feery	Bruno Lesieur
Craig Penn	Dan Levy	Dan Sheerin
Eric Texier	Frederic Durand	Gabriel White
Gavin Baxter	Greg Fisher	Hitesh Bharadia
Isabel Cody	John Kay	John Robert Cox
Joseph Pepper	Kieron Helsdon	Laurent Kermel
Martin Chamney	Olcun Tan	Paul Amer
Rebecca Waters	Robin Huffer	Val Wardlaw

2D Artists

Adam Gascoyne	Areito Echevarria	Ben Turner
Dave Bowman	Dave Early	David Man
Dave Phillips	Grant Connor	Hani Alyousif
Ian Plumb	Katherine Granger	Lilian Gahlin
Louise Lattimore	Mark Hopkins	Mark Pinheiro
Michael Illingworth	Murray Barber	Niki Wakefield
Pete Jopling	Pete Marin	Pete Smith
Richard Roberts	Steve Murgatroyd	Sara Bennett
Steven Barnes	Stuart Cripps	Veronica Luthcke

VISUAL EFFECTS BY ASYLUM

Visual Effects Supervisors . . . . Nathan McGuinness
David M.V. Jones
Executive Producers . . . . Blondel Aidoo
Emma McGuinness
Visual Effects Producer . . . . Lindsay Burnett
CG Producer . . . . Jeff Werner

Inferno Artists

Phil Brennan	Alex Ortoll	Marty Taylor
Mitch Drain	Mark Renton	Rob Blue
Jeff Olm	Phil Man	Elton John Garcia

CG Artists

Yuichiro Yamashita	Bela Brojek	Eric Lee
Gunther Schatz	David Santiago	Michael Hemschoot
Ivan Wolf	Ira Shain Pink	

2D Artists . . . . Patrick Kavanaugh
Marc Nanjo
Visual Effects Editor . . . . Kristopher Kasper
Head of Technology . . . . Tommy Hooper
I/O . . . . Brian Cuscino
Video . . . . Steve Muangman

Camera Systems, Grip & Electrical Equipment by . . . . .
ARRI / Munich
Post Production Sound Services . . . . Soundelux
Re-Recording Stage Services . . . . . Todd Studios West
Color Timer . . . . Robert Kaiser
Negative Cutter . . . . . . Buena Vista Negative Cutting
End Titles by . . . . SCARLET LETTERS
Camera Dollies for Additional Photography by . . . .
Chapman/Leonard Studio Equipment, Inc.

Services in Morocco by . . . . 3rd Cinematografica

Cast

Eversmann . . . . Josh Hartnett
Grimes . . . . Ewan McGregor
McKnight . . . . Tom Sizemore
Hoot . . . . Eric Bana
Sanderson . . . . William Fichtner
Nelson . . . . Ewen Bremner
Garrison . . . . Sam Shepard
Kurth . . . . Gabriel Casseus
Wex . . . . Kim Coates
Schmid . . . . Hugh Dancy
Durant . . . . Ron Eldard
Beales . . . . Ioan Gruffudd
Yurek . . . . Thomas Guiry
Smith . . . . Charlie Hofheimer

Pilla . . . . Danny Hoch
Steele . . . . Jason Isaacs
Harrell . . . . Željko Ivanek
Matthews . . . . Glenn Morshower
Wolcott . . . . Jeremy Piven
Kowalewski . . . . Brendan Sexton III
Shughart . . . . Johnny Strong
Busch . . . . Richard Tyson
Struecker . . . . Brian Van Holt
Gordon . . . . Nikolaj Coster-Waldau
Cribbs . . . . Steven Ford
Waddell . . . . Ian Virgo
Twombly . . . . Thomas Hardy
Galentine . . . . Gregory Sporleder
Goodale . . . . Carmine Giovinazzo
Joyce . . . . Chris Beetem
Thomas . . . . Tac Fitzgerald
Sizemore . . . . Matthew Marsden
Blackburn . . . . Orlando Bloom
Othic . . . . Kent Linville
Ruiz . . . . Enrique Murciano
Maddox . . . . Michael Roof
Atto . . . . George Harris
Mo'alim . . . . Razaaq Adoti
Firimbi . . . . Treva Etienne
Somali Spy . . . . Abdibashir Mohamed Hersi
Briley . . . . Pavel Vokoun
Fales . . . . Dan Woods
Wilkinson . . . . Ty Burrell
Goffena . . . . Boyd Kestner
Jollata . . . . Jason Hildebrandt
Somali Kids . . . . Kofi Amankwah
Joshua Quarcoo
Somali Father . . . . Johann Myers
Somali Son with Gun . . . . Lee Geohagen

Stunt Coordinator . . . . Phil Nielson
2nd Unit Stunt Coordinator . . . . Keith Woulard
Assistant Stunt Coordinator . . . . Andy Martin

Stunts

Pavel Bezdek	Ales Bousi	John Collett
Eugene Collier	Gergely Csolle	Eric Etje
Jiri Firt	Michal Grun	Rene Hajek
Jan Holicek	Peter Hric	Rob Inch
Charles Ingram	Roman Jankovic	Klaus Jindrich
Ratislav Kotula	Miroslav Lhotka	Branislav Martinak
Tomas Peterac	Lubomir Misak	Louis-Marie Nyee
Peter Olgyay	Jan Petrina	Austin Priester
Jaroslav Psenicka	Stanislav Satko	Marek Toth
Martin Uhrovik	Miroslav Valka	

Soundtrack on Decca/UMG Soundtracks

MUSIC

"Tall King Dub"
Written by Raz Mesinai
Performed by Badawi
Courtesy of Reachout International Records, Inc.
(R.O.I.R.)
By arrangement with Ocean Park Music Group

"Ul iyo Dirkeed"
Written and Performed by Omar Sharif

"Suspicious Minds"
Written by Mark James
Performed by Elvis Presley
Courtesy of The RCA Records Label, a unit of BMG
Entertainment
Under license form BMG Special Products

"Barra Barra"
Written by Rachid Taha and Steve Hillage
Performed by Rachid Taha
Courtesy of Mondo Melodia/Barclay

"Right Turn"
Written by Jerry Cantrell
Performed by Alice In Chains
Courtesy of Columbia Records
By arrangement with Sony Music Licensing

"You're The Devil In Disguise"
Written by Bernie Baum, Bill Giant and Florence Kaye
Performed by Elvis Presley
Courtesy of The RCA Records Label, a unit of BMG
Entertainment
Under license from BMG Special Products

"Die Born"
Written by Travis Meeks
Performed by Days Of The New
Courtesy of Geffen Records
Under license from Universal Music Enterprises

"Gortoz A Ran – J'Attends"
Written by Denez Prigent
Performed by Denez Prigent & Lisa Gerrard
Courtesy of Barclay France
Under license from Universal Music Enterprises

"Jump Around"
Written by Erik Schrody and Larry Muggerud
Performed by House of Pain
Courtesy of Tommy Boy Music

"Creep"
Written by Scott Weiland, Dean De Leo, Robert De Leo
and Eric Kretz
Performed by Stone Temple Pilots
Courtesy of Atlantic Recording Corp.
By arrangement with Warner Special Products

"Falling To Pieces"
Written by Michael Bordin, Roddy Bottum, Bill Gould,
James Martin and Michael Patton
Performed by Faith No More
Courtesy of Slash Records/London-Sire Records Ltd.
By arrangement with Warner Special Products

"Dhibic Roob"
Written and Performed by Omar Sharif

"Voodoo Child (Slight Return)"
Written by Jimi Hendrix
Performed by Stevie Ray Vaughan
Courtesy of Epic Records
By arrangement with Sony Music Licensing

"Minstrel Boy (Film Version)"
Arranged by Joe Strummer, Scott Shields, Martin Slattery,
Richard Flack and Tymon Dogg
Produced by Scott Shields, Martin Slattery, Richard Flack
and Joe Strummer
Performed by Joe Strummer and The Mescaleros
Joe Strummer and The Mescaleros appears courtesy of
Hellcat Records

Filmed on location in:
Sale and Rabat, Morocco

Based on the series of articles originally published in *The
Philadelphia Inquirer*

Footage from "The Jerk" Courtesy of Universal Studios
Licensing, Inc.

Footage from "The Last Of The Mohicans" Courtesy of
Twentieth Century Fox Film Corporation

The Director and Producers wish to thank and acknowledge the contributions of the following:

His Majesty King Mohammed VI
The Government of Morocco
The Governor and the People of Sale
Centre Cinematographique Marocain

We gratefully acknowledge the support and cooperation of the Department of Defense and the U.S. Army in the making of this film:

Philip Strub
Special Assistant for Entertainment Media

Major Andres Ortegon, USA
Project Officer

Office of Chief of Public Affairs, Los Angeles
Kathleen Carham Ross

The Joint Staff Special Operations Directorate
United States Special Operations Command
United States European Command
Special Operations Command, Europe
United States Defense Attache Office, Morocco

United States Army Special Operations Command
United States Army Special Forces Command (Airborne)
75th Ranger Regiment
160th Special Operations Aviation Regiment (Airborne)

And our special thanks to:
General Henry H. Shelton, U.S. Army (Retired)
Former Chairman, Joint Chiefs of Staff

Color by TECHNICOLOR   KODAK

DOLBY   SDDS   DTS

RELEASED BY

COLUMBIA PICTURES
A SONY PICTURES ENTERTAINMENT COMPANY

Rating: R; Intense realistic graphic war violence and language
Running time: 143 mins.

ABOUT THE FILMMAKERS

RIDLEY SCOTT, one of the most honored filmmakers of our time, has enjoyed extraordinary success with two back-to-back international hits, *Gladiator* (nominated for 12 Academy Awards® and winner of the Oscar®, Golden Globe, and British Academy Award for Best Picture of the Year) and the box office sensation, *Hannibal*. Scott's other films—some of them among the most influential in the medium's history—have included *Alien*, *Blade Runner*, *Thelma and Louise*, and *Black Rain*.

JERRY BRUCKHEIMER is one of the most successful producers of all time, whose films have become ingrained in popular culture and have earned over $12.5 billion in film, television, video, and recording receipts. Among his motion pictures are the Memorial Day 2001 box office smash hit *Pearl Harbor*, *Remember the Titans*, *Gone in 60 Seconds*, *Enemy of the State*, *Armageddon*, *Con Air*, *The Rock*, *Crimson Tide*, *Days of Thunder*, *Top Gun*, *Beverly Hills Cop*, and *Flashdance*.

KEN NOLAN, the screenwriter, was born in Portland, Oregon, and received a bachelor's degree in English at the University of Oregon. He moved to Los Angeles in 1990, working as an assistant to various film industry executives and producers while simultaneously teaching himself screenwriting. He sold scripts in 1994, 1996, and 1998, which went unfilmed, with *Black Hawk Down* representing Nolan's first work to come to the screen.

MARK BOWDEN is the author of *Black Hawk Down: A Story of Modern War*, published by Atlantic Monthly Press in 1999 to critical acclaim. Also the author of *Bringing the Heat* and *Doctor Dealer*, Bowden has been a reporter at *The Philadelphia Inquirer* for nineteen years and has won many national awards for his writing, including the Overseas Press Club's Hal Boyle Award for Best Foreign Reporting for his original series on the Battle of Mogadishu, which has appeared in ten newspapers across the nation. Bowden has also written for *Men's Journal*, *Sports Illustrated*, *Playboy*, *Rolling Stone*, *Parade*, and other magazines.